Praise
Life is a Highway

What does God want with you, for you, from you? Ian Byrd answers that question with wisdom, grace, and clarity: God wants you to become a highway He can travel on. The image, strange at first, is both biblical and hopeful—that the God of Heaven and Earth wants nothing less than wide open access to every part of your life. Ian not only makes the case powerfully, but he shows practically how you can join God in preparing your life for just such access. This is a vitally important book and an urgently needed message.

MARK BUCHANAN
Best Selling Author of *The Rest of God*

Ian's pastor's heart is clearly seen in this book! He shares his own experience of his journey with Jesus as he follows God's road map for his life, sharing practical biblical truths to help us avoid hitting the ditch, finding the purpose we were put on this earth for, and staying focused on that. Get ready to take an adventure and go on a road trip with Ian. Enjoy the ride!

GREG MUSSELMAN
Minister At Large, The Voice of the Martyrs/ Co-host of 100 Huntley Street

Ian Byrd is one of the most passionate leaders I know. He is contagiously positive in his approach to life and has a unique way of bringing out the best in others. In his new book *Life is a Highway*, he brings a highly accessible message for anyone that seeks to discover the will of God and live up to their full potential. We have been friends for over twenty years and I have always appreciated the genuineness and openness in how he communicates. You never have to read between the lines as he has learned how to share the profound truths of God's Word in a practical and reproducible way.

MARK HUGHES
Senior Pastor, Church of the Rock, Winnipeg, Manitoba
Author of *A Greater Purpose*

With Ian Byrd's encouraging pastor's heart and countless examples of God's faithfulness, *Life is a Highway* provides practical next steps toward a deeper and more fruitful life with God.

> DR. STEVE A. BROWN, President, Arrow Leadership
> Author of *Leading Me: Eight Practices for a Christian Leader's Most Important Assignment*

Ian has captured the Christian journey with the metaphor of a highway. His humorous stories and heart wrenching experiences make this book a *must read* for those who are serious about the journey of faith. The Christian experience is full of speed bumps, accidents and broken-down rides along the road of life. When we learn to follow the GPS from our heavenly Father, we realize that the highway of life is part of the adventure of reaching our final destination. I would echo that I have experienced many of the life lessons that Ian has gone through in his journey. I pray that you take the time to read this road-map for life's journey and also take time to reflect on the "Points to Ponder" questions as you continue to your heavenly destination.

> NEIL CAMPBELL
> Family Foundations Canada (FFI) National Coordinator

The essence of Ian's journey with Jesus as a man, a husband, father, and minister is captured powerfully in this incredibly honest, transparent, engaging, and impacting book. It is a rich source of challenge and inspiration to any man or woman whose heart has been captured by God to pursue His calling and purposes in God.

> BEN GOODMAN
> Pastor of Leadership Development, Prayer and Prophetic Ministry, at Manna Church, Fayetteville, North Carolina

Within these pages, you find a man, Ian Byrd, who is transparent, who has been broken, tested, tempted, and challenged in faith, life and ministry, and has come out on the other side with his eyes fixed on One Man—Jesus. While life has often taken him through difficult and untamed territory, his goal, as should be ours, is to regain and keep a proper perspective as we journey through. While many often wonder if it's really true that God can work all things together for good for those who love Him, you can find the answer here—a resounding *yes*! If the highway you've traveled on has been, or is, rocky, windy, or still under construction, this book is for you. But don't just read it as another "nice" story or "good book;" grab a hold of the practical advice, take the time to ask the hard questions, and "set your heart on pilgrimage ... until you appear before God in Zion."

Antonio Baldovinos
Founder Global Prayer House Missions Base and Pursuit Movement

Our friend and pastor Ian Byrd shares his journey in a wonderful way, giving teaching and encouragement through stories, Scriptures and many life lessons and experiences.

The Holy Spirit, through Ian, asks questions to ponder and apply at the end of each segment of his and Val's journey. This book is for anyone on this highway of life.

Peter and Donna Jordan
Directors of YWAM Associates International

I loved Ian Byrd's new book, *Life is a Highway*. It is filled with wisdom, practical steps to discipleship, and is a cracking good read. Interwoven with Ian's own story, he manages to apply biblical truth with humor, humility, and honesty. The writer's integrity shines through and challenges you to apply scripture in every circumstance of your life. Authenticity in the Church has been critiqued in recent days so Ian's openness and vulnerability are as refreshing as they are reassuring. The helpful questions at the end of each chapter mean this book would be ideal for group study and discipleship one on one. Many books tell you what to do; this one shows you how to do it without beating you up. You'll fall in love with the book and Ian's easy style, but above all, with the author. I thoroughly recommend *Life is a Highway*. Buy ten copies and give them away. Do that and you'll have new friends for life.

PAUL REID
Pastor Emeritus, Christian Fellowship Church
Belfast, Northern Ireland

Using the analogy that is the title of the book, *Life is a Highway*, author Ian Byrd offers practical advice and inspiration to encourage us to make wise choices on our spiritual journey. That the author chooses to be vulnerable and real in his own struggles and victories adds credibility to what he has to say. If you are looking to rekindle your faith and move ahead in your devotion to God, then this motivating and encouraging book is for you.

DAVID MACFARLANE
Former Director of National Initiatives for Billy Graham Canada
Author, Speaker, and Member of Luis Palau Evangelists Network

I have known Ian for many years and been a friend and father-figure. So, it was a joy for me to read his book and reflect on the practical wisdom drawn from his relationship with Jesus and his years of pastoral leadership. His own desire to be obedient to the truths he is teaching makes *Life is a Highway* all the more poignant and believable.

Ian and Val have also been through a LOT of challenges in their lifetime and this book tells the story of how they worked through those difficulties to turn them into spiritual, emotional, and physical victories.

Ian is also very practical in this book and it's clear he's learned how to help people (and his church family) "do" and not just "know." He writes with an easy-to-read style and captivating flair that communicates his heart to bring people closer to Jesus. His down-to-earth fashion and honest writing is punctuated with morsels of humor that help us see Ian is a practitioner and not a head-in-the-clouds expert. I love that he tells so many stories and that he does it so well!

GRAHAM BRETHERICK, Registered Psychologist
Author of *Healing Life's Hurts* and *The Fear Shift*

There is no one size fits all remedy for life, however, *Life is a Highway* has much to offer everyone. I recommend reading this book devotionally and then revisiting it on occasion. Every chapter touches a milestone on our own life's highway. Ian's candid approach reveals much about our own lives and challenges you to embrace God's love, grace, and strength.

TED SERES
President/CEO at OneBook Canada

Communicating through the relevance of defining personal life experiences, combined with gifted storytelling and spiritual understanding, Ian Byrd opens up a treasure of insight as you pass through your valley of Baca (weeping) and make it a place of springs. You will find this book speaking directly to your life in diverse ways as you identify with Ian's journey with the Lord, and how He works all things together for good. Captivating, transparent, humorous, comforting, instructional, faith building, and transforming are all words to describe this Spirit-inspired mirror into Ian's life and yours.

DR. LEN ZOETEMAN
Vice-President of Canadian Fellowship of Churches and Ministers (CFCM)

Ian is a city colleague and a delightful person to know. His openness, honesty and vulnerability regarding his life's journey is refreshing, inspiring and a story to be told. Pertinent life principles were unpacked in such a practical way, like a precision tool that could benefit each user. A repeat question frequently came to mind: with what audience would this book have its greatest impact? I thought initially, individual impact, but upon further musing I feel this book could be used to stimulate excellent small group interactive dialogue that could facilitate healing and bring wholeness to many—as the answers to the questions in each chapter are unmasked, understood and applied. Enjoy your highway journey.

KENNETH GILL
Ripple Effect Ministries, Calgary, Alberta

With open vulnerability and transparency rare in today's society, Ian shares his personal experiences—challenges, twists and turns, potholes and joyous wind in his face—on his highway of life with God. Balanced by clear explanations and principles from Scripture, this book is a joy to read, leading to deep personal reflection and practical application.

Ian, thank you for opening up your life and drawing us into a deeper walk with our Father.

WAYNE JOHNSON
CEO, Tearfund Canada

Life is a Highway is an absolute must-read if you're serious about serving God. Ian Byrd's transparent and gritty head-on approach is not the standard fare you'd expect from a seasoned Christian pastor. There's an edgy tenderness to his honesty that wouldn't let me run and hide. It challenged me but it also made me laugh and cry.

JOHN SYRATT
Minister-at-Large, Claresholm, Alberta

Ian Byrd weaves together powerful Scriptures with his own unique journey to bring comfort, insight, and hope to those wanting to finish their own race well.

JASON HILDEBRAND
Actor & Creative Catalyst

I loved this book! From the moment I started reading it, I found my heart coming alive with new hope! Ian Byrd is just like most people who will pick-up this book—a sincere sojourner who authentically wants to live the Christian life to the full, but who at the same time, is conscious of his or her own weakness. Ian has revealed his life-long quest to experience the goodness of God in the midst of real life. Ian pulls back the curtain of his own journey with incredible transparency that will invite you to enter into your own reality with renewed courage. Each chapter is rich with life altering lessons that reveal how God's intention is present in every situation. I found myself taking copious notes, weeping, praying, and realizing how much I was being encouraged walking through the terrain in my own heart. Without a doubt, any fellow sojourner on this highway of life who longs to travel the full length of one's own destiny, helping others along the way, will find fresh life, hope, and authentic timely wisdom within these pages. I highly recommend it.

BRANT REDING
Lead Pastor UChurch, Every Nation Canadian Director

In *Life is a Highway*, Ian trains the reader how to find God in our everyday world. The writing seems spontaneous—we are drawn into the drama as if we are part of the event—and learning together. Each chapter makes us hungry for another real-life illustration that teaches and empowers us to become more intimate with our God, and more effective in our life's journey. Join the adventure! Develop the ability to recognize divine direction in the circumstances of life. Truly, "Life is a Highway."

DR. PHIL NORDIN
President: Equip International

Ian Byrd's book, *Life is a Highway*, is a wonderful collection of deep spiritual truths coupled with a transparent and innocent revelation of Ian's heart as he grappled with making those truths a solid fabric of his foundation. You will not be disappointed—in fact, you will be gently reminded of ancient truths as they burst through the lens of a young boy becoming a young man who becomes a seasoned friend of Jesus—tested in the crucible of life. I highly recommend this account of a "Trophy of Grace" to new believer and seasoned Christ follower alike. The gentleness of our loving Father is effortlessly woven into every chapter on a journey that leads each of us home. I have deep affection for Ian, and this book only augments that affection!

LEONARD HAYS
Fatherheart Ministries

LIFE IS A HIGH- WAY

Peter + Laurie,
   Thank you for your
friendship and may the
Lord bless your journey!

PSALM 84:5

LIFE IS A HIGH- WAY

A ROADMAP FOR YOUR JOURNEY

IAN C. BYRD

⚐ FORERUNNER
PRESS
CALGARY, ALBERTA, CANADA

Forerunner Press
Calgary, Alberta, Canada

ISBN: 978-1-7751405-0-4 (printed)
ISBN: 978-1-7751405-1-1 (ebook)

Editors: Jocelyn Drozda, Randi Short, John Syratt
Cover design: Jeff Gifford
Interior Design: Beth Shagene

I dedicate this book to:

My wife Valerie—best friend, greatest encourager, and strongest supporter. We've been through a lot together, but the Father has always drawn us closer to Himself and to each other. I'm so thankful I get to journey through life with you!

Our four sons, two daughters-in-law, and three grandchildren—Addison; Russell and Paola (Titus, Ephraim, and Keziah); Cacey and Lauren; and Lyndon. You are our greatest legacy, and we're excited each of you is following the highway God's mapped out for your lives.

Contents

Acknowledgments

I wish to thank:

Author Bill Perkins whom God brought into my life during the early stages of writing this book to help me adjust my style to include more stories and creative elements. Ultimately, *Life is a Highway* is much better because of him.

Author Mark Buchanan, whom God connected me with in the mid-stage of development to help spur me on to completion.

Randi Short, for providing the initial edit and invaluable feedback.

Author Jocelyn Drozda, for her priceless assistance with composition, editing, and much needed encouragement at crucial times.

Author Jeff Barnhardt, who provided the wisdom and guidance for publishing and promoting this work.

My good friend John Syratt, for his editing and vital critique.

Theo and Hilde Koehoorn, who allowed me to use their beautiful cabin in Idaho as I wrote portions of this book.

Paul and Diane Hartsook, who let me hang out at their acreage during times of writing and editing.

Every person mentioned in these pages who was a part of our journey and added so much to our lives. Thank you!

Finally, and most importantly, my Lord and Savior Jesus Christ, who has been my constant companion for every mile of my life journey. I'm so glad I will continue knowing His sweet friendship for all eternity!   IAN BYRD

Foreword

I HAVE KNOWN IAN BYRD FOR MORE THAN TWENTY-FIVE YEARS and have had the privilege of seeing him grow into an incredibly fruitful minister of the gospel. He's a true "son in the faith" and I'm continually blessed by the richness and depth of camaraderie we experience together. In this book, he invites you to participate in that same rich fellowship.

As you will soon discover, he has walked through a lot of adversity yet made each challenge a stepping stone to ever increasing victory. I really like Ian's humility and honesty—that he's always willing to examine his life through the lens of God's Word and the perspective of his family and friends. It's one of the secrets of his overcoming life and now he's willing to share those insights with you.

You are going to enjoy *Life is a Highway!* Ian's a good writer and this book has a flow that makes for easy, enjoyable reading. As he shares stories from his journey, he does a masterful job of weaving in truths that you can readily apply to your own life. I could hardly put the book down because so many of his scriptural insights and life lessons applied to my own experiences.

At the end of each chapter are "Points to Ponder" that I found very helpful as I used this book to examine my own life in the light of Ian's journey. I encourage you to also use *Life is a Highway* devotionally as it will help you gain the most from the truths and insights presented.

May the Lord inspire and equip you as you read this book. Enjoy!

PASTOR DAVE WELLS
Team Leader
LifeLinks International
Fellowship of Churches

Introduction

IT WAS THE TRIP OF A LIFETIME FOR A NINE-YEAR-OLD—SEVEN days squabbling with my older brother Peter as we endured the summer heat in the back of our non-air-conditioned 1972 Toyota Corolla station wagon; and seven nights sleeping in small, stuffy "mom-and-pop" motels along the way. It was also seven days of glorious scenery—from the seemingly endless trees and rock of the Canadian Shield in Ontario to the golden crops of the prairies, the towering majesty of the snow-capped Rockies, and culminating in the green lushness and pounding surf of the West Coast.

In July 1974, my family drove the nearly 3,000 miles from our home in Southern Ontario to Vancouver, British Columbia. Amazingly, the trip was completed using just one thoroughfare— the Trans-Canada Highway. As the longest national road in the world, this nearly 5,000-mile ribbon of asphalt connects St. John's Newfoundland to Victoria, British Columbia, and every province and territory in between.

By the time I traveled the Trans-Canada, changes had already been made to its original construction of the late 50s early 60s. Portions had been widened to accommodate increased traffic; curves had been modified to become safer at higher speeds; whole sections had been replaced in favor of straighter and more direct routes.

For some reason, such changes were fascinating to my brother and me. Realizing we were on a newer section of the roadway, we would seek out the original route. Once located, Peter would exclaim, "There's the old road," and we would begin to follow its snaking path—often running nearly parallel to the new thoroughfare; other times disappearing temporarily through trees or rock formations. The new section was at places only a couple of miles long, while at others it went for ten miles or more. At some points, the old highway was still in use as a secondary road while elsewhere it was closed entirely—grass and brush beginning to poke through the bulging and cracked asphalt.

In between games of "I spy with my little eye," which my mother would initiate to try and break the monotony (why couldn't in-car DVD players or *Game Boys* have been invented thirty years earlier?), I would stare out my window and marvel at both God's creation and the amazing efforts needed to construct a highway through it.

I could imagine work crews laying explosive charges and blowing off whole rock faces in Northern Ontario so a narrow ledge for the road could be created between a towering cliff and the hundred-foot-drop to a rushing river below. Near Boston Bar, British Columbia, I was fascinated by a series of tunnels blasted through the mountains—asking my dad to honk our car horn in each one so I could hear the sound reverberate on the stony walls as we traveled through (a simple pleasure for a kid).

I could also imagine the early settlers who didn't have the luxury of such a fine roadway—bumping along on dirt paths in their covered wagons, finding their way cross country through trial and error. I realized we've certainly come a long way since those days.

This same stretch of road was again relevant in my life, when, in my early 40s I lived just off the Trans-Canada. From my kitchen window, I often watched the movement of vehicles, ranging from motorcycles, cars and vacation RV's, to the largest eighteen-wheelers.

My history with highways perhaps explains why one of my

favorite passages in the Bible is in Psalm 84 (NIV84). Verses 5 to 7 say:

> *Blessed are those whose strength is in you,*
> *who have set their hearts on pilgrimage.*
> *As they pass through the Valley of Baca,*
> *they make it a place of springs;*
> *the autumn rains also cover it with pools.*
> *They go from strength to strength,*
> *till each appears before God in Zion.*

Through many difficult times, this passage has helped me regain and keep a proper perspective about my days on this earth; I'm only passing through. I have journeyed and will yet traverse some deep valleys, but ultimately I will become stronger and stronger until one day I finish my course and meet Jesus.

This interpretation is certainly correct, but if we look more closely at this passage, a powerful word picture becomes apparent.

The American Standard Version reveals this nuance in verse five where it says, *"Blessed is the man whose strength is in thee; In whose heart are the highways to Zion."*

In this version, and indeed in the original Hebrew, the implication is not just that people have set their hearts on a lifelong journey to glory, but that they have determined their lives be so transformed by God that they become filled with the *highways* He uses to transport His power and grace to a hurting world.

The Message paraphrase also illustrates this picture:

> *And how blessed all those in whom you live,*
> *whose lives become roads you travel;*
> *They wind through lonesome valleys, come upon brooks,*
> *discover cool springs and pools brimming with rain!*
> *God-traveled, these roads curve up the mountain, and*
> *at the last turn—Zion! God in full view!*

Wow! I don't know about you, but this picture excites me! God wants to prepare my life so it becomes a highway on which *He* can *travel*. I am to be a conduit of His presence in this world—my heart becoming a spiritual turnpike to God's dwelling place.

Just as the Trans-Canada highway was built through difficult and untamed territory, God must also build His highways through the difficult regions of our lives.

The Prophet Isaiah describes this process:

> *"In the desert prepare the way for the Lord;*
> *make straight in the wilderness*
> *a highway for our God.*
> *Every valley shall be raised up,*
> *every mountain and hill made low;*
> *the rough ground shall become level,*
> *the rugged places a plain.*
> *And the glory of the Lord will be revealed,*
> *and all mankind together will see it.*
> *For the mouth of the Lord has spoken."*
> (Isaiah 40:3–5 NIV84)

Although this passage is predicting the ministry of John the Baptist who prepared the way for the coming Messiah, it also illustrates the Lord's desire that our hearts and lives become straight highways through which He can move.

Before I ever studied this passage, the Lord gave me a powerful picture during one of my toughest life seasons—a picture I now realize relates to this Scripture. This difficult period was one of emotional, economic, and physical turmoil as I tried to start and operate a magazine publishing business. Facing financial ruin, I was holding onto promises from God that I would have a successful and fruitful life—a reality appearing extremely remote.

One evening as I drove home from another seemingly wasted day trying to sell advertising for my new publication, the Lord gave me a mental picture. It was of a large superhighway filled with traffic about six lanes across. Not only were there cars and pickup trucks, but the roadway was also traveled by large eighteen-wheelers carrying immense loads. It was impressive. Incredibly, I heard the Lord say to me, "That is what your life is to be like." At that moment, my life seemed more like a goat path to nowhere than it did a first-class superhighway.

The Lord continued by showing me all of my trials and difficulties were actually a process facilitating the construction of this roadway in my life. A large and effective highway requires elaborate preparation if it is to withstand the weight and strain of thousands of pounds of moving steel and varying weather conditions. I sensed that if I wanted the level of fruitfulness God had planned for me, then I would have to endure the painstaking road preparation He had prescribed.

After that night, my pressures and strains didn't change markedly, but my attitude certainly did as I realized persevering through my difficulties would have a desirable and lasting effect. The Lord was busy building a Trans-Canada-like highway through my life, for His glory.

This book examines this very two-fold concept—how God builds His highways in our hearts and lives, even as He directs and guides the very journey, or highway, we travel in this life. We'll examine how to make spiritual growth a priority, even amidst the distractions of life's urgent demands. We'll determine the keys to transforming our difficult moments into times of renewed strength, expectancy, and encouragement as we draw closer to the Father heart of God and come to understand His goodness. We'll learn how to become *better* as we wait and as we persevere, even when circumstances pull us toward bitterness and cynicism. Finally, we'll explore how we can finish strong and leave a legacy, avoiding the pitfalls that trip us up and prevent us from running hard to the finish line.

Are you ready to start on our journey? Let's roll!

1

THE START OF THE JOURNEY:
Facing Facts

THE RAIN BEGAN TO QUIETLY FALL ON THE HEAVY PLASTIC laid on the ground for our night under the stars. *Oh, no,* I thought. *This can't be happening. Surely we won't have another wash-out.* I was 17 and in my third week as a counselor at a children's ranch. We had comfortable cabins to sleep in, but Thursday night was the open-air campout in a valley near the ranch. The guys would sleep on one hill, the girls on the other, with a *no man's land* in between.

For my first two weeks, Thursday was a rainy day and we didn't even attempt to go to the valley. On the third week, the sun shone brightly in a clear blue sky, so the campout was a "go." Excited chatter filled the air as I led my 12-year-old charges to the valley, toting our sleeping bags and gear. Conditions began to change just before we rolled out our bags onto the plastic. Like wolves lying in wait, dark, threatening clouds rolled in and unleashed their fury. The light patter of raindrops turned into a downpour.

Until that point, I had believed I was having an amazing spiritual impact on the boys in my cabin. Each day we had devotions where I shared from the "wealth" of my 17-year-old spiritual experience. This consisted of a solid religious foundation, as I grew up in a Christian home and received good teaching from my parents and the churches I had attended. However, there were some areas in which I was still a bit shaky. One of these was my understanding of how to live by faith and believe God for things like finances or healing.

Looking back, I realize I took the teachings of certain prominent ministers out of context and, regrettably, my cabin became the recipient of my wrong understanding. For example, when one of the boys came down with a cold, I told him he wasn't sick but was merely experiencing lying symptoms. He looked at me, sniffing his runny nose and wiping his watery eyes and insisted, "I'm sick!"

Anyway, back to the campout. As the rain pelted our sleeping bags and drenched our clothing, one of my disciples spoke from the deep reservoir of truth I was depositing daily. "It's not raining!" he yelled mockingly. As I stood with drops falling down my face, the absurdity of that statement hit me. Our denials wouldn't change the circumstances. We could pray and ask the Lord to stop the rain, but we couldn't alter conditions simply by ignoring they existed. We needed to acknowledge the weather was bad but then look to God for help.

The same was true for the young man with the cold. He wouldn't be healed just because we denied his sickness. We needed to admit he was ill but recognize God's provision for health through the death of Jesus on the cross. The Bible says, "by his wounds we are healed" (Isaiah 53:5). Our faith is in God's promise to us and should not be dissuaded by current circumstances. Again, we acknowledge present conditions but pray in faith for change.

I wish I could find that kid and thank him for his timely sarcasm. That one statement, spoken at the start of a torrential downpour, began to unravel my tangled belief system. I learned there's a clear difference between living in denial—ignoring reality and choosing to believe all is well even when circumstances say otherwise—and exemplifying an attitude of faith, which is complete trust and confidence in God's promises, despite outward conditions. This uncompromising faith is our first point of interest as we begin examining life's highway.

Abraham is a good example of a true faith-filled life. When he was 75 years old, the Lord told him to leave his homeland and journey to a new country, Canaan, which he and his descendants would inherit. At the time, Abraham and his wife Sarah did not have a child. When it comes to birthing a child, 75 is already old (Sarah was likely about 64), yet God allows the situation to degenerate even further before He fulfills His promise. It isn't until Abraham is 99 and Sarah nearly 90 that God tells them they'll have a son within the year. If I were Abraham, I'd be looking at myself in the mirror, glancing over at my beautiful but aged wife, and then shaking my head in despair.

Amazingly, Romans 4:18–21 says Abraham continued to believe in spite of their physical condition:

Against all hope, Abraham in hope believed and so became the father of many nations, just as it had been said to him, "So shall your offspring be." Without weakening in his faith, he faced the fact that his body was as good as dead—since he was about a hundred years old—and that Sarah's womb was also dead. Yet he did not waver through unbelief regarding the promise of God, but was strengthened in his faith and gave glory to God, being fully persuaded that God had power to do what he had promised.

Abraham "faced the fact that his body was as good as dead," but he believed God's promise anyway—that's faith! The Lord is looking for the same trust and confidence from us. I like what blogger Darryl Baker writes about verse 19: "Another way of saying this is that Abraham did not allow what he knew to be true in the natural to be the focus, instead he focused on what God had told him and he did so by keeping his thoughts in line with that Word. Walking by sight happens when we allow our natural senses to dictate to our minds what we are going to think about or focus on. To walk by faith, we must instead choose to focus our attention on God's Word."[1]

I want to use the acronym RISE to help us remember four key principles from this passage to help us see our faith increase even in challenging times:

R – FACE REALITY

Rather than walk in denial and ignore his weakened physical state (that he was old and his body was not functioning as in his youth), Abraham chose instead to embrace reality but still believe God was greater than any limitation and would fulfill His promise. As mentioned previously, we too must *face the facts* of our situation before we can begin to move in faith.

For example, if we want to see our finances increase and debts reduced, we must admit our present condition. How bad is my situation? Is my present course leading me to greater financial health or toward debt and insolvency? Embracing the truth is always vital.

I – STAY INSISTENT

This Romans passage says Abraham *"did not waver through unbelief regarding the promise of God."* In other words, despite negative circumstances, he remained insistent God would do what He said. He refused to give in to the doubts and uncertainty that tried to fill his heart and mind.

To follow Abraham's example of faith, the questions to ask ourselves are, "When I encounter obstacles to the fulfillment of God's promises, how quick am I to give up and let go? Do I quickly yield to perceived defeat or do I insist on standing firm no matter how things appear?"

We can only remain in this state of insistence if we keep God's Word front and center in our lives. To do this, there are three practices I believe are *essential* for all of us:

1. Speaking God's Word

Romans 10:17 says, *"So then faith comes by hearing, and hearing by the word of God"* (NKJV). There's something about hearing truth that stirs faith in our hearts and helps us continue believing despite negative circumstances. I have prayer cards I regularly use to declare Scriptures regarding such things as healing, the availability of God's wisdom, and the certainty of my divine destiny. Speaking these passages reminds me of God's faithfulness and rebuilds my confidence in Him.

Joshua 1:8 says *"This Book of the Law shall not depart from your mouth, but you shall meditate in it day and night, that you may observe to do according to all that is written in it. For then you will make your way prosperous, and then you will have good success"* (NKJV). As Joshua prepared to lead the Israelites into the Promised Land and faced the corresponding pressure and obstacles, the Lord reminded him to speak God's Word all the time (don't let it depart from your mouth).

The Lord knew Joshua would be tempted to become discouraged and even demoralized as he began facing the armies of Canaan. The antidote, however, was for Joshua to constantly speak and declare God's promises for the Israelite people. Those were more real than the immediate circumstances. Likewise, we too must daily remind ourselves of God's promises if we are to walk through our lives with faith and confidence.

This passage in Joshua also highlights the second practice:

2. Meditating on God's Word

The Lord tells Joshua to meditate day and night on Scripture—continually considering and thinking about its meaning. In some religions, meditation involves emptying one's mind of all thoughts. The biblical practice, however, involves keeping Scripture front and center—turning that passage over in your mind and considering its multifaceted meaning. It also can be likened to a cow chewing its cud so it can be digested and the nutrients absorbed. Likewise, when we meditate on Scripture, we're breaking it down so we can ingest its life and truth and receive spiritual nourishment. Through this convention, our faith is fed and our confidence in God increases.

Finally, verse eight shows us the third practice:

3. Acting on God's Word

"This Book of the Law shall not depart from your mouth, but you shall meditate in it day and night, that you may observe to do according to all that is written in it. For then you will make your way prosperous, and then you will have good success" (NKJV).

God is telling Joshua the end result of speaking and meditating on Scripture is the faith to act and obey. The same is true for us. Practicing these two disciplines helps us be insistent to observe and obey what the Lord has told us to do and, in the end, results in success and prosperity.

So, **R** – face **R**eality; **I** – stay **I**nsistent; the third key principle to helping us increase our faith, even in challenging times, is:

S – BE STRENGTHENED

After Abraham refused to give up on the Lord's promise, he was *"strengthened in his faith and gave glory to God."* His faith and confidence grew after he resisted the temptation to quit. What could have been a defining moment of despair and resignation became a time of spiritual growth as Abraham pushed through to a deeper faith by refusing to give in to his feelings. Likewise, you and I are strengthened when we accept reality but then insist on believing God's promises. Our strength is built and we can begin worshipping the Lord and celebrating the anticipated answer to prayer.

In the summer of 2010, my wife Val and I experienced such a strengthening by a promise God had given me. It was at this point we were preparing to leave The Bridge in Medicine Hat, the church we were pastoring, to pioneer a new church in Calgary. It was only five months until we planned to leave the city, but we still didn't have a replacement pastor. We had looked at various options but nothing had worked out.

One day a truth stood out as I read the story of Moses and the burning bush in Exodus. As Moses argues with his call to lead the Israelites into the Promised Land, he tells God he's weak and an ineffective speaker. God responds by saying He will send with Moses his brother Aaron. In fact, God tells Moses that Aaron *"is already on his way to meet you"* (Exodus 4:14).

When I read that phrase, I sensed the Lord applying that to our situation. We were worried about who would lead our church once we had left, but God was saying He had it covered and someone was already being positioned to assume that role. I was strengthened in my faith and confidence as I latched onto this promise. I shared this concept with the other members of our church leadership team and the phrase "Aaron is on his way" became our rallying cry to trust in God's provision.

True to His Word, God led our good friend Richard Klok, along with his wife Margaret, to move to Medicine Hat and become lead pastor. The Lord had put a desire for change in their hearts and was steering them bit by bit toward *The Gas City* (as Medicine Hat is called). Aaron had truly been *on his way.*

E – REMAIN **E**XPECTANT

In the end, Abraham was *"fully persuaded that God had power to do what he had promised."* He was convinced that not only had God promised him and Sarah a son in their old age but also was absolutely confident the Lord had the power and ability to follow through on that commitment no matter how bleak circumstances appeared. This type of expectancy is a byproduct of the first three steps: facing reality, insisting God's promises are true, and being strengthened in faith. Ultimately, we persist because we're *sure of what we hope for and certain of what we do not see* (Hebrews 11:1).

To allow God to build His highways in our hearts and lives, we must start by facing our current condition. Denying reality and spiritually sticking our heads in the sand is not living by faith. However, if we face facts and believe the Lord is able to mold and prepare us for future growth, we'll see Him respond to that faith and ultimately fulfill His promises as we persevere.

POINTS TO PONDER

1. Are there any *realities* in your present circumstances that the Lord is challenging you to accept but then look to Him for change?

2. Are there any places in your spiritual walk in which you need to be insistent? What promises must you cling to, and how can you use the Word of God to bolster your resolve?

3. What past successes can you celebrate in which you refused to give up on a promise and therefore were strengthened in your faith? How might that encourage you now?

4. In what areas do you have an expectation God will powerfully do what He has promised?

PRAYER

"Dear Lord, I thank You for Your challenge and encouragement to change. I realize at times I've not faced the facts about things in my life. I've sought to deny problems exist and instead pretended everything's alright. I come to You now to admit my weakness and my need for Your intervention. I'm facing facts that in my own strength I cannot see Your purposes fulfilled in my life. Forgive

me for being proud of my own abilities and depending upon my own limited resources rather than upon You. I choose instead to trust in Your strength and ability so You can accomplish all You've planned for me. I commit myself afresh to You and ask You to please show me any areas where I'm not "facing facts." In Jesus' name, Amen."

2

REST STOPS AND TRAFFIC SIGNALS:
Waiting on the Lord

I STOOD WITH THE OTHER PEOPLE GAZING IN AWE AT THE three eagles slowly circling the bay in front of the island, catching updrafts, gradually rising higher and higher into the clear blue sky. These majestic birds were ascending effortlessly against the backdrop of sunlit, snow-capped mountains on British Columbia's west coast.

I was at the Barnabas Retreat Centre on Keat's Island (a half hour by boat from Vancouver) acting as mentor for three participants in the Arrow program—a premier ministry for developing Christian leaders. It was already a gorgeous morning but seeing the eagles was icing on the cake; an exclamation mark at a time when God was highlighting a Bible passage involving these very same powerful birds.

This vein of revelation started just prior to my birthday that year when my brother gave me a book by Andrew Murray called *Wings Like Eagles*. In the work, Murray examines a portion of Isaiah 40, calling us to wait on God and be renewed in our strength.[1] The Scripture passage concludes,

> *Have you not known? Have you not heard? The everlasting*
> *God, the* LORD, *The Creator of the ends of the earth, Neither*
> *faints nor is weary. His understanding is unsearchable. He*

gives power to the weak, And to those who have no might He increases strength. Even the youths shall faint and be weary, And the young men shall utterly fall, But those who wait on the LORD Shall renew their strength; They shall mount up with wings like eagles, They shall run and not be weary, They shall walk and not faint" (Isaiah 40:28–31 NKJV).

Amazingly, the following week I had heard others either reference Isaiah 40, or mention eagles in some context almost daily. Then, the night before my trip west, I was having dinner with my extended family and I received a belated birthday card from my brother and sister-in-law. In keeping with Deb and Les' healthy sense of humor, the card was a comical tribute to old age. Tucked under their signatures, however, was something a little more serious and spiritual—*Isaiah 40:31*. There it was again! God was definitely giving me a significant signpost to point me in the right direction—highlighting a key principle that would help me navigate my future journey.

By the time I arrived in Vancouver, just before the five days of Arrow training, the passage in Isaiah 40 (waiting on the Lord, getting fresh strength, and soaring on wings like eagles) was therefore very much heightened in my awareness. During the bus ride from the airport, I shared the string of "eagle events" with Steve Brown, now President of Arrow Leadership. "Isn't it amazing, Steve," I said, "that God keeps bringing eagles and that Scripture passage to my attention!" He nodded and expressed some amazement but didn't comment much further. I later realized his response was muted because he didn't want to tip his hand about the nature of an upcoming Arrow assignment.

After breakfast the next day we gathered briefly to receive a devotional card inscribed with a Scripture passage and meditation questions. Without noting its contents, I took the card and retreated back to my room. After settling into a comfortable chair, I paused for a moment before looking at the assignment. *With what's been happening lately,* I thought, *I bet the passage in Isaiah 40 is on this card. That would be an amazing confirmation of what God's been saying!*

I flipped the card over, and ... YES! It was that very passage! God was clearly speaking to me. I spent the next few minutes excitedly considering again the Scripture that was becoming very familiar and deeply encouraging.

As the allotted time wound down, I left my room and returned to the meeting area for debriefing. I neared the building and Steve suddenly stuck his head out the door. Looking toward the bay, he said to me, "Have you seen the eagles?"

"No, what do you mean?" I replied.

"While we've been meditating on Isaiah 40, eagles have been soaring over the bay," he said with a smile on his face. "Look!"

Turning around, I joined several others taking in the majestic scene I described earlier. Later I was told an eagle sighting was rare, making the coupling of their appearance with the devotional certainly more than coincidental. It was a thrilling object lesson the Lord arranged to reinforce His desire for us as leaders to wait upon Him and be refreshed.

After watching the eagles swoop and climb in the bay, I decided to head back to my room. Capping off the whole experience, I suddenly noticed an eagle perched on top of a tree—its snowy white head, folded wings, and imposing outline high above me. Just when I thought it couldn't get any clearer, here was one last reminder of the message God was speaking to my heart. God knew I needed that exclamation mark as I headed into the next season of my life.

The following year-and-a-half was intense. My family and I transitioned from leadership of The Bridge church in Medicine Hat, Alberta, after a decade of ministry, and in May of 2011, we moved to Calgary. Then finally, after much prayer, planning, and effort, we launched Church of the Rock Calgary in January 2012. It was a whirlwind of change and I can see why God highlighted the passage in Isaiah 40—only through *waiting* could we survive and then thrive in this transition process.

Feeling overwhelmed and unprepared to start a new church, it was vital we depend increasingly on God's strength and grace; in our weakness, we had to learn to attach ourselves to His greatness. In essence, this is the meaning of the Hebrew word translated *wait* in Isaiah 40:31: "to bind together" (perhaps by twisting strands as in making a rope).[2] I interpret this to mean slowing down and taking the time to focus on God and His strength is like binding ourselves to His immeasurable might and ability.

The Hebrew meaning of *wait* also implies having a confident expectation—to "hope" or "look expectantly."[3] Waiting on God is not a passive activity but rather the anticipation of something special because we know who God is and what He can do.

This reminds me of the excitement I felt each time we waited for and anticipated the birth of one of our four sons. After nine months, we were finally going to see the little midnight kicker face-to-face. What would he (or she) look like? Each birth was a special moment and always gave me a sense of awe and wonder as I witnessed a new life entering the world. I had to be careful with my pre-birth exuberance, however, because my wife Val was in a great deal of discomfort and her *waiting* was certainly more intense than my own. Too much eager celebration at the wrong moment might trigger an elbow to the ribs, or something even worse. Thankfully it never came to that.

Val's *waiting* required her to focus on the imminent joy of seeing our new baby rather than her current discomfort and labor pains. This enabled her, literally, to push through that difficult time and see the birth of a new life.

We needed to have a similar focus between the completion of our Medicine Hat ministry and the birthing of Church of the Rock Calgary. In the middle of that period, the Lord used some good friends to encourage us in our *waiting*. As Luke and Amanda Eicher, Lead Pastors of Grace Church in Sturgis, Michigan, prayed for us at our annual church network conference, Amanda told us we were going through a number of "sunsets" in leaving our Medicine Hat church family but were soon to experience a season of "sunrises" as we started Church of the Rock Calgary.

That picture resonated with me. When the sun sets, its light rays and influence on the day gradually decreases as it slowly descends toward the horizon. As the light diminishes, darkness increases. Finally, the sun becomes a faintly glowing orange disk just above the horizon one instant, and then suddenly . . . gone. The day has ended and now begins a wait, in darkness, for the dawning of the next.

Leaving Medicine Hat certainly felt like that sunset. During the transition process, as we watched the sun gradually set on our pastoral ministry at The Bridge, sadness and grief filled our hearts. Then, following the transition service where we set in Richard Klok as Senior Pastor, ten years of ministry was abruptly over. What followed was a night season of transition, shadows, and waiting—a necessary *time between times* preparing us for our next assignment as we determined to expectantly trust in God's promises and wait for the dawning of a new ministry day. We were living Psalm 130:5–6, *"I wait for the LORD, my whole being waits, and in his word I put my hope. I wait for the Lord more than watchmen wait for the morning, more than watchmen wait for the morning."*

As the late J. Hampton Keathley III, pastor for 28 years and occasional teacher at Moody Bible Institute, wrote in his article, *Waiting on the Lord*, "When we, like the guards of the city, wait for the morning, we are waiting for more than simply time to pass. We are waiting for the sun to rise and day to break, for the light to replace the darkness, and the cold to be replaced with the warmth of the sun."[4]

With waiting often comes weariness. However, the antidote to this fatigue can be found back in Isaiah 40:31: *"But those who wait on the LORD shall renew their strength; They shall mount up with wings like eagles, They shall run and not be weary, They shall walk and not faint"* (NKJV). Those who wait on the Lord are no longer weary because they "renew their strength," which means to restore or replenish.[5]

When my iPhone begins to get "weary," the first warning I receive on my screen reads "20% of battery remaining." If I persist in using the phone and don't plug it into a power source, I get a second warning, "10% of battery remaining." If I still don't respond, a short time later the phone suddenly goes black, and I've lost all communication. Plugging the phone into an electrical source, however, begins a replenishing process and eventually my iPhone battery is restored to 100%. Its strength is renewed, and now I can text, talk, take pictures, check out Facebook, soar on the wings of technology ... (okay, too far).

Likewise, when I first realize I'm becoming weary in my waiting or even in my service to God—faithfully working at my job, trying to meet the emotional and physical needs of my wife and children, serving in my church or ministry—I need to heed the warning and take the time to plug in to God's grace and the power of His Holy Spirit through worship, prayer, and reading the Word. Delaying just makes me weaker, and eventually I'll completely run out of spiritual charge.

Ephesians 5:18–20 says, *"Don't be drunk with wine, because that will ruin your life. Instead, be filled with the Holy Spirit, singing psalms and hymns and spiritual songs among yourselves, and making music to the Lord in your hearts. And give thanks for everything to God the Father in the name of our Lord Jesus Christ"* (NLT).

In the original Greek language, the phrase "be filled with the Holy Spirit" actually means "be being filled." In other words, it isn't a one-time act but rather a daily pursuit to be filled by God's Spirit through reading and meditating on His Word, worshipping, and giving thanks to Him. Just like my iPhone needs a daily plug-in and recharge, Christians need a regular refreshing and replenishment of strength by the power of the Holy Spirit.

According to Isaiah 40:31, those who pursue this renewal *"shall mount up with wings like eagles. They shall run and not be weary. They shall walk and not faint.*" In other words, they will rise above the weariness caused by the fast-paced pressure of the unexpected, the emergencies, and fatigue to the point of fainting caused by the constant grind of completing boring, tedious tasks—they will rise above the problems and stresses of life. Such everyday living can wear us down and make us weak unless we're regularly refreshing our spirits and allowing the Holy Spirit to inject us with His joy and excitement.[6]

Waiting on the Lord cultivates an attitude of absolute dependence on Him—a posture He blesses and empowers. Jeremiah the prophet writes, "*The LORD is good to those who depend on him, to those who search for him. So it is good to wait quietly for salvation from the LORD*" (Lamentations 3:25–26 NLT).

Such a mindset of dependence truly is a complete reliance on God's strength and ability. This was exemplified to me as I watched those powerful birds on Keat's Island. It was amazing to see how effortlessly they ascended. They weren't madly flapping their wings in a wild effort to gain height. In fact, they didn't seem to be doing anything except positioning themselves to catch the powerful thermal updrafts so they could gradually climb higher and higher. Likewise, we need to stop our *harried flapping* through life, and in a posture of waiting, position ourselves to catch the powerful updrafts of the Holy Spirit to be carried above the unexpected and the mundane of daily living, into the heights of faith and confidence in God.

G. Campbell Morgan, pastor of London's Westminster Chapel for periods during the first half of the 20th Century wrote:

> "Waiting for God is not laziness. Waiting for God is not the abandonment of effort. Waiting for God means, first, activity under command; second, readiness for any new command that may come; third, the ability to do nothing until the command is given."[7]

POINTS TO PONDER

1. In what areas are you waiting expectantly for the Lord?

2. Are there any areas where you perhaps should be waiting on the Lord, but are struggling to do so?

3. How can you include replenishing moments in your life in which you connect with God and are recharged in your faith?

4. How can you incorporate the practices of Ephesians 5:18–20 into your life so you can regularly be filled with the Spirit and know the Lord's strength and joy?

PRAYER

"Dear Lord, I thank You for Your promise to renew my strength as I wait upon You. I no longer want to "harriedly flap" my way through life but rather desire to learn how to rise up effortlessly on the updrafts of Your Spirit. In areas where I fall short, give me the wisdom to know how to draw near so I can be replenished and refilled with Your Holy Spirit. In Jesus' name. Amen."

GOD'S GPS NAVIGATION:

Choosing the Better Thing

MARTHA'S MIND RACED, HER BODY IN CLOSE PURSUIT, AS she rushed around the house preparing a perfect dinner for the special guest: Jesus of Nazareth. *I wonder how dinner's coming. Is everything cooking properly? How's the atmosphere of the house? Is it clean, orderly, and dusted? Is my guest comfortable as He waits for the meal to be served?*

Pausing from her harried preparation, she checked on Jesus. A quick glance confirmed He was relaxed and enjoying himself. *That's good!* But there at His feet, hanging on His every word, sat Mary! *We can't sit around doing nothing,* Martha thought. *If Mary started helping, we could get things ready more quickly, Jesus could be enjoying a delicious meal sooner, and I wouldn't be working so hard and feeling tired and stressed.* As she continued rushing about, these concerns and feelings bounced around her mind like a bumble bee trapped inside a house—constantly hitting the windowpane while looking for a way out.

Finally, Martha could take it no longer. She dumped her frustration on Jesus: *"Lord, don't you care that my sister has left me to do the work by myself? Tell her to help me!"* (Luke 10:40).

Martha waited for an affirming response from the Lord. Certainly, He would see the unfairness and encourage Mary to help her, saying, "Let's talk later, Mary. Your sister needs your help now, and it's only right for you to give her a hand."

That's not how it played out. Jesus empathized with Martha's stress but challenged her to follow Mary's example: *"Martha, Martha," the Lord answered, "you are worried and upset about many things, but few things are needed or indeed only one. Mary has chosen what is better, and it will not be taken away from her"* (Luke 10:41–42).

I can imagine Martha's thoughts as those words sank in. *You mean You would rather I ignore all these important matters and join my sister in sitting at Your feet? What about dinner? What about making sure I do things right for You and making sure my actions are befitting the great King and Messiah? I don't understand!*

It's easy for me to use poetic license in telling this Bible story because I can relate so well to Martha's plight. Like her, I often struggle to separate my ministry for the Lord from my ministry to Him—from rushing around doing necessary Kingdom tasks to spending time in His presence listening to His voice. I know some people think all a pastor does is pray, worship, read his Bible, and prepare a message for the Sunday service—the one time a week he actually produces something significant. I wish! As lead pastor of a growing church, I wake up each day with a long list of things to accomplish: people to connect with, difficulties to troubleshoot, administrative duties to complete. Sitting before the Lord, reading His Word, and waiting to hear from Him can seem like a delay to these important tasks. We need to shift away from this mentality and understand that it is in these pit stops where we are supplied with the food to energize us for the journey, fuel to keep us moving forward, and the map to keep us on the right road. It is only through these crucial pit stops that we are properly equipped for our travels so we're not left stranded by the side of the highway.

If I'm not careful, my mind and spirit become consumed with the daily work I need to do, and I begin to lose focus on Him. Before I know it, I'm replying to emails, writing out my *to-do* list, and my time of waiting is gone. I've quickly shifted from Mary to Martha—from rest to stress. One moment I'm sitting at Jesus' feet listening intently to His wisdom and encouragement; the next I'm up off the floor and hurriedly moving to another task. I can just imagine the look of bewilderment on His face as He wonders, *Where are you going? What are you doing? I had some other things to share with you. I wasn't finished!*

The problem is, when I start running and working like Martha, I also start feeling like her: busy, stressed, envious of the peace and restfulness of others, angry, frustrated. In the previous chapter, we contemplated the importance of waiting on the Lord. Now, using the story of Mary and Martha, I want to unlock the reality of another dimension to waiting—communion with the Lord in prayer.

The Bible says such prayerful waiting is the antidote to the tension and stress I described earlier. Isaiah 64:4 says, *"For since the world began, no ear has heard and no eye has seen a God like you, who works for those who wait for him!"* (NLT). That's a good trade-off; we wait on Him like Mary, and He intervenes on our behalf.

I'm like Martha more than I want to admit, but I'm learning to slow down and listen. As I do, I find I live and work in greater peace throughout the day. Like Mary, I must first choose the *better thing* if I'm to avoid the stress and frustration of Martha.

To further remind me of this truth, a framed print representing a somewhat modern-day version of this Bible story hangs in my office. In this picture, set in the 1940s or '50s, judging by the vintage telephone and furniture, a middle-aged, graying businessman sits behind his desk in suit and tie. His chair is turned to his right, left elbow on the tabletop bearing the weight of his head as it rests against his hand. In his right hand, he holds his eyeglasses close to his chest as he focuses earnestly on Jesus, who's sitting opposite him. The Messiah, with long brown hair, beard, white robe with red sash, is gesturing with His left hand as He explains something to the man. Underneath the picture is Psalm 1:1 in the King James Version, *"Blessed is the man that walketh not in the counsel of the ungodly, nor standeth in the way of sinners, nor sitteth in the seat of the scornful."*

I can't tell you how many times this image has encouraged me to go back to Jesus for the answers needed to lead our church. The businessman obviously knows who the real head and leader of his enterprise is, and chooses to walk in His counsel and guidance. Like Mary, the executive is choosing to first seek the wisdom of his Lord before engaging in the busyness and complexity of running a corporation. Some days he's running hard to adjust to emergencies and unexpected difficulties, while on others he's struggling to stay interested and alert as he methodically deals with the regular, predictable tasks of corporate leadership.

Either way, spending time with the Lord and receiving strength and guidance is the cornerstone of his daily routine and the key to his continued success. This drawing on my wall implies the businessman has ongoing dialogue and discussion with the Lord rather than a prayer list in which he recites a monologue that must be as boring for the Lord as it is for the one giving it.

I believe God wants us to be real with Him in our times of waiting and prayer. My conviction stems from an experience similar to the businessman in the print. Growing up in a Christian home, I gave my life to Jesus at age six, after my mother read me a bedtime story. I had never had much spiritual fervency, however. I was a nice, clean kid who didn't swear and who tried to obey his parents and teachers, but beyond that, I lacked the passion to even read the Bible or pray on the most basic level. I was riding the coattails of my parents' faith.

That all changed at sixteen when I sensed a growing hunger for God. My Bible, which I had rarely cracked open, suddenly became my favorite literature. With an orange highlighter in hand, I began reading through the New Testament and marking passages that particularly spoke to me.

My sudden awakening even caught my mother off guard. As a pastor, she was responsible for leading several Bible studies. One evening she was running late for one of those meetings and, unable to find her own Bible, grabbed mine and headed out the door. Later, during the study, I was told she was so surprised to see my orange highlights she blurted out to the whole group, "My son's reading the Bible!"

Along with my voracious appetite for Scripture, my desire to pray became an unquenchable thirst. Arriving home from high school, I'd immediately head to the basement where I'd usually spend about two hours in worship, prayer, and Bible study.

My prayer style was, perhaps, unorthodox. Rather than kneeling, folding my hands and closing my eyes, I would sit cross-legged on the bed, eyes wide open, talking with God as if He were actually in the room—as one friend might converse with another. I didn't know any different, and that was probably for the better. I would worship, share the details of my day, and then pray for the needs of others. It was very fluid and informal.

As time went by, however, I began to have nagging doubts that maybe God wasn't so pleased with my casual approach and might be offended by my lack of more formal, pious behavior. *Maybe I should start kneeling,* I thought. *Maybe God isn't even listening because He thinks I'm not really serious about my relationship with Him.*

However, these concerns were put to bed (pun intended) at a youth Bible study one night. As I entered the gathering, Sue, the co-leader, said to me, "Ian, I'd like to talk with you afterward. I think I have a word from the Lord for you."

That may sound unusual, but the Bible is clear that one of the spiritual gifts is prophecy—the Holy Spirit giving people impressions and ideas for strengthening, encouraging and comforting others (1 Corinthians 14:3) to build them up in their faith. Sharing such prophetic messages with others is possible when Christ followers learn to wait on the Lord and listen for His voice. (I will share practical tips for this process shortly.)

I was excited to hear the message, so I approached Sue almost immediately after the last amen. Heading downstairs, we stood in the recreation room as she told me two things: "Ian, the Lord really likes the way you pray, and He also wants you to know you're going to be a man of God."

Wow! How did she know about that? I wondered as I considered the part about prayer. I hadn't told anyone of those concerns, least of all Sue. *This must truly be a message from God! Everything's okay. He likes the way I pray. HE LIKES THE WAY I PRAY!*

It was clear God enjoyed my times with Him, and the fact I was also called to "be a man of God"—a person who represented His character and power—was icing on the cake. The doubt and pressure were gone because I knew the Lord liked my intercession.

My cross-legged prayer experience was the teenage equivalent of the businessman's meeting with Jesus. Now, in my middle age, it's key I rekindle and retain that innocence and simple faith as I spend time praying and seeking Him. As I do so, the cares and concerns of this world become smaller and my sense of His greatness increases.

Having such experiences for yourself is paramount and can be achieved by waiting on God through listening prayer. This is vital because, as I mentioned earlier, hearing God's voice is a tremendous encouragement and strength for ourselves and for others.

The first way to practice such prayer is through the use of Scripture. The Benedictine Monks (established 590 AD) developed a Bible meditation method called Lectio Divina—Latin for "divine reading." Since this discipline has greatly helped me in hearing God's voice, I want to share a version of it with you.

The first step is selecting a portion of Scripture to read (usually not more than ten verses to start with). Once you settle on that passage, take a moment to invite the Holy Spirit to speak to you through it.

Next, read the passage through once or twice, asking God to highlight a word or a thought as you read, and then write this in a journal. At times, I also write down the entire passage as I seek to internalize it within my mind and spirit. After again reading the Scripture slowly, ask the Lord to show you how your life is touched by this passage, and then write your impressions in the journal.

After this, read the whole passage at least once more, and ask God if there's an invitation for you within it. Is He welcoming you to trust Him in a new way, change your way of thinking, or maybe take a bold step of faith in your walk with Him? Again, write down your impressions.

Finally, use the Scripture to pray about whatever God has brought to your mind. This prayer might be for you, other people, or for a particular situation. It could be requesting something from God, praying for someone else, confessing your sin, or even offering up thanksgiving. Bottom line: as you listen to the Holy Spirit, He will turn the Scripture into an effective prayer for you and others.[1]

Recently, I was using this method on a Sunday morning as I prepared for another service at Church of the Rock Calgary. This particular day I was feeling discouraged about some church matters *(yes, pastors do have some down moments)* and needed to hear God's reassuring voice again. I chose to read Joshua 1:1–9 where, after the death of Moses, God encourages Joshua as he prepares to lead the Israelites into the Promised Land.

After reading the passage a few times, a couple of phrases leaped off the page at me. Twice God tells Joshua to "be strong and courageous" (verses 6 & 9), and one time he ramps it up to "be strong and *very* courageous" (vs. 7). It's adamantly clear the Lord will enable Joshua to boldly and effectively lead the Israelites as he carefully obeys God's Word. The second standout phrase was God declaring to Joshua, "You are the one who will lead these people" (vs. 6). Because God chose him, Joshua could be confident the Lord would make Him successful.

As I read this passage and focused on these two phrases, I sensed the Holy Spirit touching and strengthening my heart. My discouragement began dissipating as I was reminded God chose me to lead my church and He wanted me to be strong and courageous as I moved forward in His purposes. I needed to remember that, as I continued obeying the Lord's leading and direction, our church would take new "land" for His Kingdom.

After receiving this revelation, I concluded by declaring these truths in prayer and believing for a great, God-honoring service. My spirits were lifted and my heart encouraged because I heard God's voice as He spoke to me through His Word.

A second way to practice listening prayer is through journaling our dialogues with God. I find this is most effective after spending time worshipping the Lord, unloading my burdens, and putting my focus squarely on Him, in an environment without distractions.

Once your heart is prepared, the next step is writing out your prayers as questions. This is where the issues of your heart become an invitation for the Lord to provide His solutions and guidance. For example: "Lord, what is the key to me overcoming the anxiety I feel?" or "What should I do in this situation?" You may also ask the Lord to give you an encouraging message for a friend or family member that you can share with him or her later (a simple way to procure prophetic words for others). Wait in silence and begin to write the first thoughts that come to mind in reply to the question asked. These answers may spark further questions as you allow the Lord to probe and guide your heart. Also, it's exciting having a permanent record of your dialogue with God and going back through journal entries much later, reminding yourself of what the Lord had said and being spiritually refreshed once again.[2]

The question often asked as people begin this process is, "How do I know if what I'm sensing and writing is from God?" This is a valid concern and I want to give you three ways to assess what you're writing.

First, nothing God says to you will ever go against His revealed Word as recorded in the Bible. The objective truth of Scripture trumps the subjective nature of your journaling every time.

Second, ask a mature brother or sister in Christ to help you discern what you're hearing. As Bob Japenga, a Christian leader who guides individuals and groups through prayer retreats, writes in his book, *An Introductory Guide to Listening Prayer*, "If God tells you to do something radical, do not act on it without the prayers and assurances of others. This is the heart of what it means to be the body of Christ, all connected to the head."[3]

Finally, the passing of time is another way to determine if what you're hearing is genuine. When you look back at your journal months or even years later, your true impressions will be highlighted, while the times you didn't hear correctly will also be apparent. As Japenga writes, "Give God time. It is very rare for God to say, "Do such and such immediately—I need your immediate obedience" in things involving major life decisions (marrying, buying a house, choosing a career, starting a ministry, etc).

Ultimately, hearing God's voice is a learned skill and we only become proficient at it as we step out in faith, begin trying, and keep trying.

In addition to listening prayer, another best practice for waiting on God is focusing on His awesome power. Psalm 52:9 says, *"In the presence of Your saints I will wait on Your name, for it is good"* (NKJV).

In keeping with the Psalmist's practice, I regularly wait on the Lord's name by praying His different titles recorded in the Old Testament—on occasions when He powerfully revealed qualities of His character. In English, the proper name for God is translated "Lord," while in Hebrew the translation is "Yahweh" or "Jehovah." Either can be used, but I prefer "Jehovah." Hence, when God reveals Himself as "The Lord Who Heals" in Exodus 15:26, I use His proper name "Jehovah-Rapha." Other titles are "Jehovah-Nissi," "The Lord our Banner" (Exodus 17:15); Jehovah-Tsidkenu, "The

Lord our Righteousness" (Jeremiah 33:16); and Jehovah-Shalom, "The Lord is Peace" (Judges 6:24).[4]

I encourage you to look up these Scripture references for yourself and read the stories surrounding them to gain a better understanding of these names. (More names and information can be found at *www.gotquestions.org/names of God.html*). Along with reflecting God's character, these names represent ways He promises to move and work in our lives. When personally waiting for God's next steps, praying these names by faith provides tremendous encouragement and strength, helping me focus on God's unlimited ability rather than on my finite weakness. I can then remain alert and in the proper mindset as I wait at His feet for His next instructions and guidance.

All that being said, like Mary we must make the better choice—the one certified by Jesus—spending much time listening and waiting at the feet of our Lord!

POINTS TO PONDER

1. In your service to Jesus are you more like Mary or Martha? How is the Lord encouraging you to be more like Mary and choose *what is better*—spending time with Him?

2. In what areas do you need to seek the Lord for His advice and counsel? How can you organize your life so you have time for prayer?

3. What is your style of prayer and how might it differ from that of others? Are you confident in the way you pray and sense God's affirmation? If not, ask Him to encourage you and show you how to make prayer a natural part of your life.

4. How can you incorporate listening prayer into your everyday life, and what is your next step to making this a reality?

5. What are the names of God that are particularly meaningful to you in this season? How can you use them to encourage yourself in your waiting?

PRAYER

"Dear Lord, I thank You that You're approachable and love to spend time with Your children. Father, You know how busy and distracted I can become at times. Forgive me when I allow that busyness—even with activities for Your Kingdom—to pull me away from praying and listening to You. Show me how to live so I can make time with You a regular part of my life. Open up my eyes and my ears to see and hear You more. Increase my desire and hunger for You. In Jesus' name. Amen."

4

CHARTING THE COURSE:
A Heart Set on Pilgrimage

OUT FOR A WALK ONE DAY I DID SOMETHING VERY UNUSUAL; I began admiring our fine city sidewalks constructed so pedestrians could safely coexist with passing vehicles. It's easy to take such a thing for granted, but for some reason on this day, I began celebrating the finely contoured white pathway so meticulously created out of concrete. Square after carefully formed square, the walkway stretched in front of me like a white ribbon between the green lawns and black asphalt.

Then suddenly, the perfect symmetry was shattered. In one of the concrete squares, a meandering tire track was visible; its tread and width firmly etched into the walkway. Immediately following was the unmistakable imprint of a running shoe—probably about size ten—a testament to someone's carelessness as they strode through the fresh cement. I recalled that at other times I'd seen a dog's paw prints pressed into a sidewalk as if the owner had wanted to immortalize Fifi for all time!

The appearance of these imperfections on this day of sober sidewalk reflection gave me pause to consider how such a picture could relate to life. Now, I must point out that though I'm a pastor, I'm not into making every circumstance some kind of metaphor, but in this instance, I did see some life application. When I began noticing the tire tracks and running shoe imprint, my initial thought was, *Oops, somebody goofed and forgot to wait for the concrete to dry … (I know, I'm Captain Obvious) … and now these marks are set in stone as a testament to their carelessness or indifference.* I considered how permanent those mistakes were, and how, for years to come, those imperfections would be visible to all.

I contrast those regrettable tire tracks and shoe imprint, however, with the intentional markings scratched in the concrete at the cabin on Echo Lake, Montana, where our family stays each summer. Inscribed in a patch of cement just outside the entrance to the workshop is the year *1968.* Unlike the tracks and imprints, the inscription was an intentional decision to commemorate the pouring of concrete and the shop's completion—still visible decades later!

One is accidental, the other intentional, but both become a permanent life record. Similarly, our hearts and lives are also imprinted like these cement sidewalks. We start out as those that are moldable and open to outside influence and change, whether intentional or not. However, our living patterns gradually become cemented in and eventually determine and set the course of our life's highway. This makes change exceedingly more difficult than if we had initially chosen the right road.

As parents, we can either be deliberate about impressing godly principles for living onto the hearts of our children, or we can allow other influences and circumstance to haphazardly do it for us. There are many individuals who would love to leave their shoeprints on the hearts of our children, and similarly, organizations and institutions that would relish indenting the *tire tracks* of their standards and ideals.

Even though the primary setting of heart foundations happens in our very early years, there is an ongoing solidification I believe happens at other key moments as well. I now realize there were some faulty foundations set into my psyche at an early age. Both of my parents were pastors in the United Church of Canada (my Mom taking over for my dad after he passed away), and therefore, in keeping with the rotation practices of the time, we moved every two to three years. Frequently being the new kid in school led to growing up with footprints of insecurity, anxiety, and inferiority on my heart—mindsets and conditions of which the Lord has been healing me as I continue walking in relationship with Him.

As I reached an age where I was responsible for my own actions and the development of my personal faith in the Lord, I had to determine how serious I was going to be about serving Him. Would I be completely committed and surrendered to Christ—fully *set* in my resolve to serve Him—or would I allow other pursuits and influences to be imprinted on my heart and draw me away? Thankfully, as a sixteen-year-old (as I shared earlier) I had made a quality decision to fully pursue God's purposes for my life. Before that time, I was a good Christian kid who had given his life to Christ at age six but lacked any true passion or hunger for the Word of God and prayer.

Sixteen was a setting point in my life—a season of awakening. When the Holy Spirit drew me to a deeper walk with the Lord, I determined I was going to accept the pilgrimage and highway building that best describes that journey. As Psalm 84:5 says, *"Blessed are those whose strength is in you, who have set their hearts on pilgrimage"* (NIV84). I had come to realize true blessing comes to those who have *set their hearts* on making life a journey. They're not content with the status quo but rather determine to see their hearts become the highways upon which God can travel.

The definition of *set* is "to fix firmly; to make fast, permanent, or stable."[1] There is no variableness in the word "set;" it is the condition of being unwavering, undaunted, unmoving and determined.

One whose heart is set on pilgrimage and has a fixed attitude toward a lifelong pursuit of God's purposes will not be deterred by difficulty or obstacles. He has a "come hell or high water" approach much like those who risked the dangers of the high seas and pioneered to settle this continent. Our best example of this mindset is Jesus Himself. Luke 9:51–52 says that as the time approached for Him to be taken up to Heaven, Jesus resolutely set out for Jerusalem. The dictionary defines resolute as "Having a decided purpose; fixed in a determination."[2] Impressively, Jesus showed such decisiveness despite knowing the torment and death eventually awaiting Him in Jerusalem. He was truly *set* on the prize of securing our salvation and freedom from death and damnation (Hebrews 12:2).

If Jesus wavered one iota in His heart, He had every occasion to abort the mission and give in to the desire for comfort and safety. The Garden of Gethsemane would have been the end of His whole pilgrimage. If Jesus had not set His will in alignment with that of His Father's, He could easily have caved in to the very real and terrifying natural pressures He experienced in that garden. Instead, He kept His focus on the bigger picture of salvation and redemption for all mankind. The short-term pain and sacrifice was a worthwhile price, considering the eternal joy of seeing countless millions of souls come to realize everlasting life.

In Philippians, Paul the Apostle tells us we are to have an identical mindset. He writes:

> *Think of yourselves the way Christ Jesus thought of himself. He had equal status with God but didn't think so much of himself that he had to cling to the advantages of that status no matter what. Not at all. When the time came, he set aside the privileges of deity and took on the status of a slave, became human! Having become human, he stayed human. It was an incredibly humbling process. He didn't claim special privileges. Instead, he lived a selfless, obedient life and then died a selfless, obedient death—and the worst kind of death at that: a crucifixion* (Philippians 2: 5–8 MSG).

Wow! That's a *set* perspective—no vacillating, no waffling. Our attitude must be the same as that of Jesus; "This is my destiny, my divine calling and I won't be dissuaded from following this path to completion, no matter what." Paul challenges us to set both our hearts (or spirits) and minds on "things above," on those matters pertaining to our walk with Jesus Christ. He implies that if we don't make such a conscious decision then other areas will compete for that attention (Colossians 3:1–4).

I'll never forget when my resolve to remain *set* in pursuing God's purposes was severely tested. I was living in Taber, Alberta in the late 90s and serving as volunteer youth pastor at New Life Church. As I share elsewhere in this book, life was challenging as I attempted to make a living as a white-collar guy in a blue-collar town. My ultimate goal was to someday lead my own church, but that dream definitely seemed a long way off.

I became impatient with the pace of the journey. I was leading the youth group, but as such, was not on the church eldership team—and definitely didn't feel in line to take over any another church. I sensed God telling me to remain resolute in trusting Him, not promote myself, wait for His timing, and be confident He would eventually advance me.

My resolve weakened, however, when I heard that Pastor Dave Wells of Harvest City Church in Regina, Saskatchewan was coming to speak at New Life and then meet with the leadership team afterward.

I wish I could be in that meeting, I thought. *Dave has such great leadership insight and it would be so refreshing to be with the others and learn from one of the greats!* After considering my options, I picked up the phone and dialed the number of Doug Shimoda, our pastor. After he answered and we exchanged pleasantries, I jumped to the heart of my request. "Doug, I heard that Dave Wells is meeting with your leadership team on Sunday. I know I'm not part of the team but was wondering if for this meeting I could attend and hear Dave?"

There was a brief pause and then Pastor Doug replied, "I'm sure that would be okay, Ian. The meeting really is for the leadership team and will deal with related matters, but I'm sure it would be alright if you joined us this once." I thanked Doug for his permission, told him I'd see him Sunday, and hung up.

For a brief moment, I was excited to attend but then began feeling uneasy as I sensed God wasn't pleased. It was as if I could hear His still small voice say, *So, are you taking charge of your destiny, Ian? Is it now up to you to find ways for your advancement? Because if that's what you want I'll stand back and let you take over!*

The thought of God taking His hands off of my development journey and leaving things up to me was very scary, indeed. I knew I would make a mess of things. With this in mind, I quickly redialed Pastor Doug's number. As soon as he picked up I said, "Doug, I've been thinking about Sunday's meeting with Dave Wells. Thanks again for your willingness to allow me to attend, however, I recognize it really is a meeting just for the leadership team. So, I won't be coming. Again, I really appreciate your openness to having me there." He graciously accepted my decision and we finished the call.

After hanging up I again heard that still small voice, but this time it said, "*Good job, Son. That was the right call. Don't worry, your day will come!*"

Obeying the Lord always brings peace, but as I was still feeling frustrated with my overall situation, after Dave Wells preached that Sunday, I grabbed Val's hand and we both headed up to the front of the church to ask Dave and his wife Linda to pray for us. As we stood with those great leaders, I shared my frustrations and feelings of disillusionment.

"Dave and Linda," I started. "I just don't know if our time will ever come. I believe eventually there will be greater leadership responsibility for Val and me, but it seems like we're getting nowhere." What followed was just the advice I needed.

"Ian," Dave said, "just as when Joseph was in the Egyptian prison and then Pharaoh suddenly called for him and he was quickly elevated to a significant position, God will eventually whistle for you and you'll be promoted. In the meantime," he continued, "I want you to make Doug look good. Serve his ministry and put all your efforts into being faithful as a youth pastor."

The advice made sense. *Make Doug look good,* I thought. *I can do that. Yeah, Dave's right. God hasn't forgotten me. If I'm faithful to my work here, He'll eventually promote me.* A new faith and hope suddenly filled my heart and I felt strengthened in my resolve. Now was not the time to give up and give in. I needed to remain *set* in my determination to do things God's way.

As an aside, Dave's advice is a principle all of us should follow—whether we're in church work or some other career or occupation. Serving our employer well and making him or her look good honors God and brings His blessing into our lives. In Colossians 3:23–25, Paul the Apostle writes, *"Whatever you do, work at it with all your heart, as working for the Lord, not for human masters, since you know that you will receive an inheritance from the Lord as a reward. It is the Lord Christ you are serving."*

In addition, when we're faithful to serve another man or woman's vision and calling, the Lord can then trust and release us to pursue our own—or as Jesus said to His disciples, "Whoever can be trusted with very little can also be trusted with much ..." (Luke 16:10a). Serving others and making them look good is therefore a vital proving ground and foundation for the pursuit of our own dreams and goals.

I'd like to say our discussion with Dave and Linda was the end of my frustration, but at various times during the months that followed, I was again tempted to take matters into my own hands. Watching the ordination and release of close friends into ministry weakened my resolve and soon another opportunity arose for me to plead my case and perhaps get my promotion train moving.

One afternoon on my way home from work in Lethbridge (a half hour west of Taber), I decided to stop and visit Dr. Keith Hazell, a spiritual father and, at the time, leader of LifeLinks International Fellowship, the church network with which I'm affiliated. As we sat on the front steps of his house basking in the summer sun and talking about life, I decided to broach the subject.

"Keith, I was wondering if there would ever come an opportunity for me to be ordained to the ministry," I said with a hopeful look on my face.

Thinking for a moment Keith said, "Well, I suppose if you had occasion to begin ministering beyond your local church it could be important for you to have the authority provided by ordination. I'll give it some thought."

Like my chat with Pastor Doug months earlier, I thanked Keith for his consideration, and after some further discussion said, "goodbye," hopped into my car, and headed home. After arriving back at my house in Taber, however, I again had that uneasy feeling in the pit of my stomach.

As before I could hear that still small inner voice saying, *So, are you taking charge of your destiny, Ian? Is it now up to you to find ways for your advancement? Because if that's what you want, I'll stand back and let you take over!* Again, I immediately realized I wasn't smart enough to assume such control. I quickly called Keith, and just like my previous discussion with Doug, thanked him for his willingness to consider my request but told him I didn't think I was ready for ordination at this time and asked him not to give it another thought. He accepted my assessment and we finished our chat.

I sensed the Lord's approval and felt like He was saying, *Don't worry Son, your day will come!*

My resolve to remain patient and wait for God's timing lasted for a time, but then my old feelings of frustration and disillusionment returned. Thankfully, this time I had a God encounter that permanently set my perspective and truly hastened my promotion.

While praying one day in mid-January 2000, I finally completely surrendered my ministry aspirations to God and humbled myself before Him. Oh, yes, I had tried doing this so many times before, but this time was definitely different. Sitting in a room at the church I suddenly said to the Lord, "If You want me to be a volunteer youth pastor here in Taber, Alberta for the rest of my days and that puts a smile on Your face, then I'll do it. I'm here on this earth to please You and make You happy. And if being a youth pastor here is what does that then I'm in!"

The cool thing was I meant every word; it wasn't an attempt to manipulate God but rather a genuine surrender to Him and a heartfelt desire to please Him alone. With tears streaming down my face it was as if the sun broke through the clouds of my soul and I could finally sense peace and rest. Gone was the striving and struggle of the past. My future was truly in God's hands and I was finally content with that. It was as if I finally allowed the Lord to fully imprint His future upon my life. I was now set and determined to follow His purposes for me, no matter how long that took or how illogical the path appeared.

Amazingly, nine months later, Pastor Doug sat opposite me at the Taber A&W and in between sips of coffee, presented the opportunity for Val and me to lead our network's church in Medicine Hat. The day of promotion had finally arrived! It's no coincidence the opportunity was presented only once I had surrendered completely to the Lord, was willing to wait for His timing, and truly *set* my heart on pilgrimage. It seems my January confession was all God was waiting for before He set our advancement in motion.

For all of us, these are days we need to make sure our hearts are set on a pilgrimage of change and spiritual maturity. We must allow God to imprint His purposes on our lives and reject the tire tracks or shoe prints of anyone or anything else. We must also consistently surrender our aspirations to the Lord—making sure our agenda is in line with His and that we're committed to waiting for His timing. Ultimately, it involves complete submission of our will and trusting He's marked out our life highway and therefore will ultimately guide us to the glorious and fulfilling destiny He has planned for us.

POINTS TO PONDER

1. Where is your heart in the process of gaining a set perspective? Are you allowing other influences to imprint their perspectives on your heart rather than seeking God's point of view? If you sense the Spirit's leading, take a moment to ask God's forgiveness and surrender your life anew to His influence and timeline.

2. Have you been discouraged or dissuaded from completely pursuing an ever-deepening relationship with Jesus? If so, what changes are needed to make this pursuit a reality?

3. What specific steps do you need to take to see this new resoluteness in your spiritual walk?

PRAYER

"Dear Lord, I realize I have not fully 'set' my heart on pilgrimage— on completely and passionately pursuing Your purposes for me. I have been unwilling to change but have instead settled and been satisfied with a mediocre Christian walk. I sense You are calling me to come up higher in my pursuit of You and I am saying 'yes' to that call. Lord, I want to be resolute in fully surrendering to Your commands and purposes even when I face obstacles and difficulties. I no longer want to give in to distractions or excuses for aborting my spiritual mission. Instead, I choose to believe You are true to Your Word and will provide and take care of all that pertains to me as I faithfully serve You. I love You Lord, and I ask You to help me fulfill this commitment by the power of Your Holy Spirit. In Jesus' name, Amen."

5

HIGHWAY WIDENING:
Practices for Inner Growth

I WAS RUNNING LATE AND THE TWO-LANE HIGHWAY FROM Taber to Lethbridge, where I worked selling advertising at a television station, was clogged with commuters and large agriculture trucks, which didn't help. Directly in front of me was a big one-ton carrying sugar beets. It was fall, and local farmers were hauling harvested beets to drop off at depots where large semis would transport them to the sugar factory in Taber. I appreciated the importance of moving such goods, but on this day, it was becoming a nuisance. Sugar beets could be seen here and there on the roadway—renegade vegetables somehow escaping from the trucks. I just hoped one wouldn't fall in front of me, potentially denting my car, or worse, causing an accident.

"Come on, come on," I muttered, willing the truck ahead of me to move faster. That wasn't going to happen, however. There were just too many vehicles for the two lanes and nothing could change that except the province widening the roadway.

Thankfully, the government was already on top of the issue and had begun a three-year project to develop a four-lane highway. During that time, the thoroughfare was widened approximately six miles per year. What a relief each fall when the barriers came down. We could finally drive on the newly-laid asphalt and revel in the fact that we had an additional portion of carefree roadway now able to more adequately handle the commuters and agricultural traffic flow. The big moment, of course, was when the final section that led into our town was completed.

Highways are important, as they allow for the movement of people and goods. If they're too narrow for the traffic flow, however, they become dangerous and increase the potential for deadly accidents. Economic and population growth also necessitate enhanced and widened roadways. Without such an adjustment, growth can peak and then begin stagnating.

The same is true with our heart highway. When God asks us to step up and serve Him in a new way, what was once an acceptable level of spiritual growth and maturity can quickly seem too restrictive and limited. We sense He wants to move through our lives in a much greater way—increasing the transport of His power, grace, and mercy to others—but we may also realize our current heart roadway just isn't wide enough.

At this crisis point, we have two options. First, we can shrink back from God's enhanced calling without even considering He can increase our capacity. We may actually despair of our current condition and decide we're just too inadequate to accept the call. Unfortunately, many Christians make this decision, and for the rest of their lives live on a plateau of minimal effectiveness and limited spiritual fruitfulness. Such a retreat grieves the Lord, who desires we trust His leading and embrace His plans for our lives. As Hebrews 10:38 says, *"But my righteous one will live by faith. And I take no pleasure in the one who shrinks back."*

Our second option is acknowledging our current inadequacy but believing that if the Lord is calling us forward, He'll provide the means of completing the task. We must "set our hearts on pilgrimage"—on pursuing God's highway construction in our lives. I'm confident your desire is the same as mine: to bring pleasure to the Lord and to choose a life of increasing maturity and fruitfulness.

I vividly recall a crisis moment when I needed to decide which option to choose: shrink back or believe for God's provision. It was the start of a new year, and as I considered everything ahead of me, I could sense fear and panic rising. My involvement in LifeLinks (the network to which our church belongs) was continuing to expand as I served on the task force of our network training school and worked with four churches as an overseer, providing counsel and support to their leaders. I was also leading a three-year-old church plant needing much attention in developing and creating structures and programs for growth. It seemed overwhelming and I felt completely inadequate for the challenge.

"You've chosen the wrong guy," I told the Lord in prayer. "I can't do this and I feel so weak and incompetent." It was like a *Dark Night of the Soul*,[1] where the future seemed unclear and I despaired in my weakness. My discouragement continued for a couple of weeks until I attended a free pastor's luncheon (we love those) and the guest speaker, Mark Buchanan, shared something that changed my perspective.

Mark talked about the *Peter Principle*. For many, that title references a concept developed by Dr. Laurence J. Peter in 1968. It states, "Employees will get promoted as long as they are competent, but at some point will fail to get promoted beyond a certain job because it has become too challenging for them. Employees rise to their level of incompetence and stay there." Dr. Peter sums up the principle with the saying: "the cream rises until it sours."[2]

Although that adage may be true, Mark gleans his *Peter Principle* from the story in Matthew chapter 14. The disciples were in a storm on the Sea of Galilee in the middle of the night. As they strained against the oars and attempted to make their way to the other shore, they suddenly saw Jesus (who didn't leave with them in the boat) coming out to them on the stormy lake.

When the disciples saw him walking on the lake, they were terrified. "It's a ghost," they said, and cried out in fear.
But Jesus immediately said to them: "Take courage! It is I. Don't be afraid."

69

"Lord, if it's you," Peter replied, "tell me to come to you on the water."

"Come," he said. Then Peter got down out of the boat, walked on the water and came toward Jesus. But when he saw the wind, he was afraid and, beginning to sink, cried out, 'Lord, save me!"

Immediately Jesus reached out his hand and caught him. "You of little faith," he said, "why did you doubt?"

And when they climbed into the boat, the wind died down. Then those who were in the boat worshiped him, saying, "Truly you are the Son of God."

(Matthew 14:26–33)

The Lord calls Peter to step out of the boat and join Him on the lake. Peter obeys and has some success in water walking before turning his eyes from Jesus to the gale force winds and gigantic waves. It's then he realizes his pursuit of Jesus' call is physically impossible, begins to sink in despair, and is only saved after crying out to his Savior.

The same is true for us as we pursue God's purposes for our lives. Mark Buchanan's *Peter Principle*, as he shared at Ambrose University, Calgary in 2015 states: "The Lord will often call us to step out into an assignment beyond our ability so he can bring us into a greater place of dependence." This dependence upon God is our place of greatest strength. When Peter stepped out in response to Jesus' invitation and call, he actually came to a place of greater effectiveness, even though he appeared to fail completely.

As I listened to Mark, tears filled my eyes and I sensed the Lord bringing encouragement to my heart. It was as if He was saying, *Ian, you feel completely overwhelmed, but you're actually in a place of great spiritual growth and enlargement if you turn your desperation into a pursuit of Me and My strength!*

My situation didn't change markedly after that day, but my perspective underwent a massive shift. I determined to turn my desperation into a pursuit of the Lord in prayer and studying His Word. I was now confident my greater dependence on Him would produce increased strength and confidence in my life. Thankfully, when we're willing to have our hearts widened, the Lord is gracious enough to provide avenues and circumstances enhancing our dependence upon Him. But then, He also provides the means for us to be spiritually expanded and strengthened.

One such vehicle He uses is the relational connection with others through our local church family, provoking us to grow. The Lord never meant for us to take our spiritual journey alone. Psalm 68:6 tells us, *"God sets the solitary in families"* (NKJV). He doesn't want His people struggling on their own but seeks to put them into families of believers where they can prosper and thrive. Your placement in a specific local church is not your decision but rather should be a step taken after hearing from the Holy Spirit. As a pastor, I am always pleased when I hear new folks in our church tell me they are joining our fellowship because they sense, above all, the Lord has called them to do so. Such a decision is not based on the existence of a good youth program, effective worship service, or a dynamic children's ministry (although our desire is to have all of these), but rather on the witness of the Holy Spirit.

The Bible further develops the importance of belonging to a spiritual church family. It says, *"Let us think of ways to motivate one another to acts of love and good works. And let us not neglect our meeting together, as some people do, but encourage one another, especially now that the day of his return is drawing near"* (Hebrews 10:24–25 NLT).

It's clear each of us has a responsibility to give thought to how we may spur (as one translation puts it) or motivate one another toward acts of love and good works. It is also clear that we must receive such spurring and motivating from others. That word *spur* evokes certain pictures and images in my mind. My city hosts the Calgary Stampede, also known as "The Greatest Outdoor Show on Earth." I recall attending the Stampede rodeo and watching the world-class bronc riders bursting out of the chutes with the intention of remaining on their wild bucking horse for at least eight seconds. If riding an unbroken horse wasn't challenging enough, to increase the difficulty of the ride and score more points from the judges, these courageous riders further provoked their broncs by stroking the spurs of their cowboy boots across the bucking animals' shoulders. The response was instantaneous as the horse was stirred to more intense action and became even more determined to dismount its rider.

Though the Lord doesn't intend for each of us to literally go around spurring other members of our church family, at least not in a natural sense, He does want us, however, to be our brother's keeper in that we watch out for his or her spiritual welfare. We need a willingness to lovingly challenge and confront when we notice the level of "love and good works" beginning to subside.

If we choose to not be part of a local church family, however, we forego such accountability in our lives and can easily fall into spiritual apathy, laziness, and possible error, without anyone noticing or caring to correct us. To describe Christians without a local church family, one of my pastors used to say, "A lone ranger is a stranger in danger!"

Another way the Lord provides for our spiritual expansion and strengthening is through mentors He brings into our lives. A mentor could be considered a counselor or guide—someone that can be trusted; similar to a tutor or coach. In essence, he or she is someone ahead of you on life's journey, who understands the skills and aptitude needed for you to succeed and is willing to show you how to grow. If this person is older, they can even become a spiritual mother or father who passes on their years of insight in a very personal and loving way.

Motivational speaker Jim Rohn famously said *we are the average of the five people we spend the most time with*. In commenting about Rohn's statement, Aimee Groth of *Business Insider* wrote, "When it comes to relationships, we are greatly influenced—whether we like it or not—by those closest to us. It affects our way of thinking, our self-esteem, and our decisions. Of course, everyone is their own person, but research has shown that we're more affected by our environment than we think."[3] When applied to having mentors in our lives this means we must choose carefully who those people will be because their acumen, or lack thereof, will ultimately have impact on our success.

Craig Groeschel, Lead Pastor of Life Church (one of America's largest multi-campus churches), also places a high emphasis on mentorship. He contends we should seek out multiple mentors in each of the main parts of our lives—spiritual, family, career, financial, etc.—but be careful how we make the request for help. Groeschel says if we specifically ask someone to mentor us they will usually say, "no" because of perceived time and schedule constraints. However, if we merely invite them to lunch, breakfast, or for a twenty-minute chat, they will likely agree—and we will have gained a mentor. He suggests coming prepared with a list of questions, being careful not to overtalk, giving the person ample time to respond, taking lots of notes, and then applying what's learned. He concludes by encouraging the use of "distant mentors." Through podcasts and books, we can learn from "the best of the best" without knowing them up close.[4]

Groeschel's approach is valid. When it comes to growing in my skills as a pastor, for example, I have several seasoned leaders as *go-to* guys, depending upon the situation at hand. Each one has a forte and a specialty; the needed skill set determines which person I call.

For example, when I'm working with a church in our LifeLinks network that's going through some church government/leadership struggles, I usually look to Pastor Dave Wells for advice—our network leader from Regina, Saskatchewan and a spiritual father in my life. On other occasions, I tap my good friend Pastor Mark Hughes of Church of the Rock, Winnipeg to help me navigate some tricky issues with my own team and leaders. Still at other times,

I look south of the border to my buddy Bryan Asay of Bozeman, Montana to help me walk through times of personal struggle and family challenges, or to Graham Bretherick of Lethbridge, Alberta—a Christian counselor who has given me fatherly advice for more than twenty years. Their involvement in my life means my capacity to lead—in our network, church, and at home—is constantly increasing and my life highway is widening so I can become a greater conduit for releasing God's grace to those I lead.

Likewise, I encourage you to not shrink back from allowing the Lord to widen your heart. We must admit our complete dependence upon Him, become part of a strong local church family, and seek out mentors to provide the challenge and encouragement needed to grow. Only then can we become a large enough thoroughfare to effectively transport God's grace and love to others!

POINTS TO PONDER

1. Where are you today in this heart-widening process? Are you aware of your need to grow and willing to acknowledge the need for some spiritual *widening* in your life? What are your next steps and in what areas do you need to focus?

2. Like Peter, is God calling you to step into an assignment beyond your ability so He can teach you greater dependence upon Him? In what ways can you practice such dependence upon the Lord?

3. Have you allowed the Lord to place you in a strong local church family where you'll be stirred to action? If not, is there a church He's leading you to join?

4. Have you solicited the help of mentors/coaches and spiritual mothers/fathers to assist in various aspects of your personal development? If not, who can you invite to be a part of this process in your life?

PRAYER

"Dear Lord. I Thank You for Your desire to increase my effectiveness and make me even more fruitful. I acknowledge I need some spiritual 'widening' and ask You to work in my heart to enlarge my capacity to love and serve You. Help me to say 'yes' to the opportunities You provide, even though they take me beyond where I've been before. May I turn my inadequacy into dependence upon You and be strengthened like never before. Place in my life mentors and spiritual mothers/fathers who can help me to grow. I also ask for the privilege of mentoring and adding value to the lives of others. In Jesus' name. Amen."

6

THE HIGHWAY TO HELL:
Overcoming Impurity

Her house is a highway to the grave,
leading down to the chambers of death.
Proverbs 7:27

The highway of the upright avoids evil;
those who guard their ways preserve their lives.
Proverbs 16:17

A
S I SAT AT MY COMPUTER PREPARING FOR AN EVENING BIBLE
class, a thought flashed through my mind: *I bet the Sears
catalog is now online.* That might seem like a very random and
harmless idea, but its root and motivation were very dangerous for
me. Back in my adolescence, when my hormones were raging and
my interest in girls peaking, the arrival of the Sears catalog at our
house was a significant event. I would immediately leaf through the
slick, glossy pages until I arrived at the women's undergarments/
lingerie section. I enjoyed gazing at the smiling and scantily clad
models but immediately afterward felt a sense of guilt and shame.

I knew lust was wrong, and thankfully, my love for God pushed
me to cry out in prayer for His help to resist such temptation and
keep my thoughts pure. It wasn't easy, but with His grace and help,
I was able to stop my catalog episodes.

In talking with other men, I realize I wasn't alone in my interest in the Sears catalog, as many shared the same excitement upon its arrival. It was the most accessible material in a pre-internet era where girlie magazines and other porn were only available by store purchase. It wasn't pornography in the general sense but was close enough. However, by 2004 internet pornography was exploding because of easy access and anonymity. It hadn't been a problem for me; I had never gone there and didn't plan to do so. I didn't even have any blocking or monitoring software on my computer.

But now as I sat at my computer in my office, the idea of an online catalog entered my mind and I could feel the tug toward that old temptation and a growing curiosity about what I might find. My heart began to pound as I replaced leafing through a glossy catalog with the click of a mouse. A few seconds later I was there, and after another click, I was in the women's lingerie section just like when I was a teenager. I couldn't believe how easy and accessible it was. After my initial exploration, I exited my internet browser, and just as before, felt the familiar feelings of guilt and shame. I immediately called a fellow leader and friend and told him what I'd done. I knew it was wrong and certainly didn't want this to proceed any further. And that was that—not.

Over the next few days and weeks that lustful tug intensified and I found myself venturing back to the internet again and again, each time going a bit deeper until I was viewing pornography. The catalog was the initial hook in my soul and the enemy just kept reeling me in until I was compromising my morals and integrity.

Each episode was devastating and I would immediately repent to the Lord and to others. My ability to begin separating from the activity was only possible, however, when I installed internet blocking and monitoring software on my computer and became accountable to other leaders on an ongoing basis. Like alcoholism, once the rush of internet pornography is experienced, I believe a person is vulnerable for the rest of his/her life. Because of that, I will always choose to have software protection on my computer; the descent into ever-increasing addiction is only just a click away.

According to recent surveys, I'm not alone in my struggles as a Christian leader. Thirty-seven percent of pastors and nearly 60 percent of Christian men admit to struggling with pornography. No longer just a problem for men, 35 percent of women also admit to the addiction.[1] This is a serious issue we cannot and must not ignore.

Internet pornography has earned itself a reputation for being the crack cocaine of sexual addiction. "It works so quickly and it's so instantly intense," says Dr. Robert Weiss of the Sexual Recovery Institute in Los Angeles. "We're seeing a whole population of clients who have never had a history with the problem, but for the first time, they're beginning one particular activity and getting hooked."[2]

Likewise, achieving the same rush from viewing porn also requires stronger and stronger stimulation. Dr. Simone Kuhn, psychologist, Max Planck Institute for Human Development, Berlin, Germany explains:

> We found that a structure called striatum or caudatum in the brain's reward system is smaller in individuals who consume a lot of pornographic material, which could mean that it actually shrinks over time, depending on how much material is consumed. As a result, the individual requires increasingly more intense and more frequent stimuli in order to maintain the feeling of reward.[3]

Porn addiction is therefore never static but rather necessitates a search for more graphic and harder pornography to achieve the same "high." None of us arrive overnight in such a place of compromise. The journey is a gradual decline of standards and behaviors over time.

If we're not vigilant, pornography can become another "highway" easily and quickly built in our hearts—one parallel to the massive "thoroughfare" the Lord uses to transport His grace through us to a hurting world. As with my catalog incident, such an alternate heart roadway starts as a small, obscure path but gradually increases in size and influence until finally its deception and the allurement of the goods it transports can exceed every other roadway.

The Bible describes this highway in Proverbs chapter 7 and the misadventures of a youth traveling that road, chronicling how he walks the street where an adulteress lives, is seduced by her alluring dress and brazen behavior and eventually spends the night with her. At the end of the chapter the author concludes, *"Many are the victims she has brought down; her slain are a mighty throng. Her house is a highway to the grave, leading down to the chambers of death"* (26–27).

Could there be a more perfect description of how sexual temptation seizes men and women and eventually leads them to spiritual and moral ruin? This "highway to the grave" is being given a major and primary focus in today's culture. The seeds of its development in the lives of men and women are everywhere and all of us are going to have to, by the grace of God, be more vigilant and determined if we're to avoid this highway's construction in our lives.

Proverbs 7 starts with the young man flirting with disaster by placing himself in the position where he can be tempted and enticed to enter that house of death. He walks in the dwelling's general direction at a bad time of day—twilight. It's the time of shadows and hiddenness where his sin might be more cloaked and clandestine. He may think he can toy with the idea of participating and then leave. He's deceived and in many ways, he's already trapped.

As with most biblical analogies, it might be easy for us to disassociate ourselves from this picture and say, "What a fool! I would never be so simple. That could never happen to me. I would never go to the house of an adulterous wife looking for a one-night stand. No problem there!" And, for most of us, that's probably true. However, let's bring it a bit closer to home.

How often do men and women in our culture—yes, even Christians—put themselves in a position where they may be tempted to morally compromise. The corner they flirt with may not be a physical location but rather a website, chat room, or a movie with some suggestive scenes. It could be repeated exposure to certain television sitcoms, allowing the onslaught of their perversion to wear down their standards day after day. Or, it could be the entertainment of lewd mental fantasies, sexually graphic romance novels, or simply telling a dirty joke.

All of it, however, is designed by the enemy of our souls to desensitize us to the beauty and holiness of God's moral purity and to encourage us to gradually, bit by bit, begin compromising our standards and slowly move down the street toward "her corner." Like the frog in the water boiling to death gradually, many believers are in danger of reaching the boiling point; their lives to be imminently destroyed by such unhealthy passions and activities.

This story from Proverbs tells us she lurks at every corner and is "brazen and brash"—unashamedly aggressive. Lust and seduction are literally that prevalent in our culture. The immediate question then is, in light of all this temptation, probably more intense than at any previous time in history, how can God expect any of us to keep our ways pure? How can we stay far away from building this highway in our lives, and if we've already struggled with porn in the past, how can we regain and maintain our freedom?

As someone personally understanding this struggle, and as a pastor counseling others in this area, I want to share keys for overcoming, including best practices from some of the fine organizations committed to helping men and women gain freedom.[4]

The first key is acknowledging you're addicted and what you're doing is wrong. This initial step recognizes the behavior is beyond your strength and ability to control and resist. It has its hook in you, and without the help of God and others, you won't be able to break free. Proverbs 28:13 says, *"Whoever conceals their sins does* *not prosper, but the one who confesses and renounces them finds mercy."*

Find someone you trust to whom you can confess your activity. This could be your pastor, close friend, or someone you look up to. Bring it out of the darkness and into the light. When I did this, my heavy burden of guilt and shame was removed, and I came into a state of mind where I could receive God's forgiveness and healing.

King David wrote in Psalm 32:3–5:

When I kept silent, my bones wasted away through my groaning all day long. For day and night your hand was heavy on me; my strength was sapped as in the heat of summer. Then I acknowledged my sin to you and did not cover up my iniquity. I said, "I will confess my transgressions to the LORD." And you forgave the guilt of my sin.

In case we're tempted to downplay the sinfulness of porn and buy into society's view that it's a harmless and normal activity, Jesus sets us straight in Matthew 5:28: *"... anyone who looks at a woman lustfully has already committed adultery with her in his heart."*

One man wrote this account of how, prior to confession, his porn addiction was draining his life away:

"My wife gradually spent more and more time with her best girlfriend across the street because I was emotionally dead inside. The life had literally been sucked out of me. I felt as though my ability to think clearly was greatly affected. I had trouble repeating phone numbers because I was consumed with guilt and shame. I gradually lost respect for my wife as a person. It was almost impossible for us to carry on a conversation. These changes occurred so gradually that I did not realize it was the pornography that was affecting me."[5]

Obviously, confession is just the first step toward freedom. Lasting change and breaking away from a deep-rooted porn addiction (involving numerous poor choices over time) will require living in a new way and moving in the opposite direction from old behaviors. This process is what the Bible calls repentance.

I like the way *Family Life* (a Christian organization committed to helping families thrive) describes this heart attitude: "Repentance means "to turn around." When you have a habit of sin in your life, it is like getting in a car and driving away from God. When you repent, you stop moving away from God and turn around to face Him, and through His power start moving toward Him again. Repentance is a sorrow that comes from realizing that you have offended the very holiness of God. You must be willing to turn away from your sin and toward the life God wants for you. If you are going to deal with your sin successfully, repentance is essential."[6]

When we come to Him with such an attitude, *"... he is faithful and righteous to forgive us our sins and to cleanse us from all unrighteousness"* (1 John 1:9 ASV). This first step begins the process of gaining freedom from the weight of guilt and shame.

The second key is making yourself accountable. In chapter 16 I discuss accountability in depth, so I will only mention it here as it specifically relates to breaking free from pornography. Everyone needs a *safe* person (or persons) with whom to share his or her struggles. James 5:16 says, *"Therefore, confess your sins to one another and pray for one another, so that you may be healed. The effective prayer of a righteous man can accomplish much"* (NIV84). Enlist a team of friends to provide regular encouragement, support, and accountability as you seek to live a healthy sexual life. Don't rely on one person; make sure you have two or more so at least one's always available.[7]

Following this guideline has been incredibly helpful to me over the years—providing confidence at least one of my friends will be there when needed. Because of their availability, a quick text is all that's often needed to break temptation's power and help me move on.

In choosing my accountability partners I look for several things. Most importantly, I want spiritually mature people with whom I can be honest and transparent within the safety and con-fidentiality of our relationship. They won't condemn me when I'm tempted, but they won't be easy on me either—always encouraging and challenging me to pursue the Lord and receive His grace in my times of weakness.

Paul the Apostle declares the importance of understanding this grace—"the unmerited or undeserved favor of God to those who are under condemnation—"[8] when he declares, *"For the grace of God has appeared that offers salvation to all people. It teaches us to say "No" to ungodliness and worldly passions, and to live self-con-trolled, upright and godly lives in this present age"* (Titus 2:11–12). It's exciting that understanding and receiving the truth of God's grace and forgiveness, even when we mess up, actually provides the resolve to live pure, Christ-honoring lives.

Another vital factor in the choice of accountability partners is that they are of the same sex as you. The intimate nature of the needed conversations could lead to inappropriate boundary lines with someone of the opposite sex. In talking with other men, I realize some of them have their wives as an accountability part-ner—sometimes exclusively. Although I don't believe husbands and wives should withhold big secrets from each other, I do think it's unwise to approach your spouse every time you're struggling with some form of sexual temptation. It's better, in my opinion, to have accountability partners who will walk with you in the every-day, and can understand the situation from the same perspective; but are also mature and wise enough to know when your spouse should be approached if the situation warrants it.

I also recommend the use of accountability software to keep your partners in the loop about your online activity. I and my four sons use "Covenant Eyes." For a small monthly fee, this organiza-tion monitors all of my internet use and sends a weekly report to my accountability partners. Knowing this fact has often stopped me from proceeding down a bad internet path. *Covenant Eyes* can block designated web pages or search topics and also provides an app for monitoring phone internet use. Other options include *AFA Filter* or *Hedgebuilders*.[9]

With the great availability of pornography, I can't fathom surfing unprotected, and urge parents to install such software on all home computers, laptops, and cellphones—especially those of adolescent (and even pre-adolescent) sons and daughters. Without taking such precautions, the plight of our children might be very similar to that of Gabe Deem who shares his story in the documentary "Rewired: How Pornography Affects the Human Brain:"[10]

> Things got really bad when I was twelve years old," he says. That's when my parents got high speed Internet. What I would do is: I would go out from middle school and go home as fast as I could and watch porn, look at whatever I could for three or four hours before my parents got home from work.

The bottom line is, young or old, we need accountability to combat this ongoing assault. As Solomon wrote in Ecclesiastes 4:9–10, *"Two are better than one, because they have a good reward for their labor. For if they fall, one will lift up his companion. But woe to him who is alone when he falls, for he has no one to help him up."* (NKJV). Let's prayerfully consider whom God has called to lift us up and provide accountability in our quest to walk in moral purity.

The third key to overcoming is study and meditation upon the Word of God. Psalm 119:9–11 (NIV84) gives us one of the biggest keys to living a holy, God-honoring life:

> *How can a young man keep his way pure?*
> *By living according to your word.*
> *I seek you with all my heart;*
> *do not let me stray from your commands.*

> *I have hidden your word in my heart*
> *that I might not sin against you.*

To walk uprightly we must keep an allegiance to the Word of God; reading it regularly, and through meditation and study, applying it to our hearts and allowing it to guide our paths.

Ps 119:105 (NIV84) says, *"Your word is a lamp to my feet and a light for my path."* The Word of God will keep us from straying onto the path of the adulterous. It will help us stay in the light and away from the hiddenness and deception that will lead us into compromise and onto the highway of destruction.

In addition, Romans 12:2 tells us, *"Do not conform to the pattern of this world, but be transformed by the renewing of your mind. Then you will be able to test and approve what God's will is—his good, pleasing and perfect will."* Porn is part of "the pattern of this world," and the only way to break free and follow God's good and holy way is through the transforming power of the Word of God. It's not enough to say "No" to porn and resist its contamination of our thoughts. We must also be saying "Yes" to the truth of God's Word and actively renewing our minds.

This is best done through Scripture meditation. In chapter three I shared a best practice for this along with other tips for effective listening prayer. These techniques are essential to accomplishing the mind renewal needed to cleanse the effects of pornography.

Dr. Ted Roberts, creator of the "Conquer Series," designed to help men break free of porn, writes that engaging in effective Bible meditation "is a supernatural process that frequently triggers a neurochemical cascade of new understanding where your mind is being renewed."[11] (I've studied this material and highly recommend it. Please go to *www.conquerorseries.com* for more details or to order the resources.)

Ultimately, the conclusion of our meditation should be a commitment of heart and will to obey what the Holy Spirit is speaking and go the way He's leading. Trying harder will never bring freedom from sexual struggles but "dedicating ourselves to that direction (from the Holy Spirit) in life will change us," writes Roberts.[12]

I've found it incredibly helpful to meditate on passages such as Psalm 51, Romans 8, James 1, Colossians 3:1–10, Ephesians 6:10–18, and John 14:15–27, to name a few. Roberts specifically encourages those struggling with porn addiction to turn off all media thirty minutes before bed and meditate on Scripture, "Because God's Word has the power to physically restructure our brain. Most of the conscious decisions we make will continue to operate on an unconscious level," explains Roberts.[13]

Authors Judah Pollack and Olivia Fox Cabane take it one step further when they write, "Your brain cleans itself out when you sleep—your brain cells shrink by up to 60% to create space for your glial gardeners to remove the waste and prune the synapses."[14] Pollack and Cabane explain that glial cells are like "the gardeners of the brain"—pulling up the weeds, killing the pests, raking up the dead leaves, as it were. To use another picture, these cells remove thoughts that are not being accessed. As you and I replace old thinking with the Word of God, those unfruitful, unhelpful, ungodly thought patterns are no longer accessed and therefore, are washed away—truly "the washing with water through the Word" as mentioned in Ephesians 5:16.

In addition to Bible meditation, I regularly quote Scriptures from an app called *Rhema*, developed by the late Pastor Wendell Smith of City Church, Seattle, Washington (available at both iTunes and Android stores).[15] It includes thirteen prayer cards containing faith-building Scriptures on various topics such as *The Lord is my Strength*, *No Fear*, and *Wisdom and the Will of God*. The *Passion for Purity* card reinforces my desire to live a godly life and protect myself from porn and other impure temptations. The thirty verses on this card have often strengthened and encouraged me. No matter your method, I encourage you to actively engage in renewing your mind with the Word of God!

The fourth key to regaining and retaining sexual purity is to guard your heart and avoid temptations. Proverbs 16:17 states, *"The highway of the upright avoids evil; he who guards his way guards his life"* (NIV84). Likewise, Proverbs 4:23 says, *"Above all else, guard your heart, for it is the wellspring of life"* (NIV84).

The key to building this highway of upright living is being proactive and using the times when we're strong to develop godly practices and increase our resolve to avoid pornography. Ken James of Films for Christ writes "A simple change of habit can do wonders in keeping you from temptation. For example, if you are most tempted when you spend time on the computer after your spouse has gone to bed, then make a commitment to stay off of the computer during that time. If you know that a certain street you drive down causes you to lust due to certain establishments on it, or prostitutes that hang around, or alluring billboards, you would be wise to travel a different route."[16]

As Psalm 119:37 says, *"Turn my eyes away from worthless things; preserve my life according to your word."*

I find it helpful to follow the advice of Stephen Arterburn in his book *Every Man's Battle.*[17] Steve says we need to retrain our eyes to "bounce away" from anything that might stimulate lust. We can't help the first glance but it's that second intentional one that gets us into trouble. The best decision, therefore, is to bounce our gaze away before we focus on any enticing scene. I do this, for example, as I walk through our city malls past "Victoria's Secret" and the other lingerie outlets. I just don't let my gaze settle as I walk through that gauntlet of stores. We also need to apply *bouncing* to magazines at the checkout line, billboards, television programming, and commercials. Since a good habit can be formed in as little as two weeks, remarkable improvement can happen quite quickly when we follow this practice.

We are wise to heed the advice of Paul the Apostle to his young protégé Timothy, *"flee youthful lusts"* (2 Timothy 2:22). Or, as someone once said, run from all enticement as if from a rabid dog.[18]

As we conclude this chapter, I encourage you to follow the steps and principles outlined above, humble yourself before God, and begin to gradually experience victories and progress day by day. As Stephen Arterburn writes, "Recovery is a cinch by the inch, but a trial by the mile."[19]

POINTS TO PONDER

1. Has the enemy of your soul been enticing you to move down the street "near her corner" and compromise your godly standards by flirting with areas of impurity and lust? If so, how can you stop the progression and put up barriers so you won't *go there* in the future?

2. To whom can you be accountable in this important area of your life?

3. In what ways can you guard your heart and avoid temptation?

4. Are you feeding your mind and spirit with the Word of God so you're empowered to resist sin and clearly see the path of holiness the Lord has for you? How can you incorporate Bible reading and meditation into your daily life?

PRAYER

"Dear Lord, I Thank You for making the way for me to be a pure and holy follower of You. Through the power of what Jesus did on the cross, I can walk in freedom and resist all temptations. Help me make wise decisions so I don't put myself in vulnerable situations where I might compromise. Show me the ways to walk in accountability, guard my heart, and feed my mind and spirit on Your Word. I thank You for Your unconditional love and acceptance of me. In Jesus' name. Amen."

7

GOD'S DETOURS:
A Pig in a Hatchback

As I DROVE TO THE DOG KENNEL I KEPT WONDERING, *How did I end up with a grotesquely fat potbelly pig in the back of my 1991 Plymouth Colt hatchback?* An hour earlier I was making (what I thought) was a routine pastoral call to pray for an elderly woman before her admittance to the hospital for treatment. In that short time, however, I'd morphed from Pastor to pet taxi driver. I was a rookie pastor, with less than a year under my belt, and none of my training had prepared me for this.

The shift in mission started soon after I drove up to Jane's (not her real name) little white bungalow in an older part of Medicine Hat known as "The Flats." In responding to her earlier call for prayer, I imagined I'd only be there fifteen minutes or so and then continue with my day.

However, her first comment after welcoming me into the house was, "You have a hatchback, right?"

"Yes," I hesitantly replied, unsure of where this conversation was going.

"Well," she continued, "I need to take Piggy Sue to the dog kennel so she can be cared for while I'm in the hospital. Would you be able to take her in your car?"

I glanced over at Piggy Sue and realized afresh what an ugly animal she was. On a previous visit, Jane told me the story of how she came to own a pet potbelly pig. She shared how Piggy Sue was, at first, such a petite animal. Jane made a mistake in feeding her, however, and rather than giving her standard pig fare (whatever that is) she accidentally fed Piggy Sue the feed commercial pork producers use to fatten their stock for market. The result was this hideous black blob—an animal so fat I was unclear how she could see or move with her swollen eyelids and almost imperceptible short, stubby legs. Nonetheless, Jane loved her and wanted her precious pet taken care of during her absence.

I thought for a second and realized, *I better help. How can I say "no" when I have a vehicle that works and Jane needs some peace of mind before heading to the hospital?*

"Sure, I can do it," I said weakly.

"Great," replied Jane as she smiled and began preparing Piggy Sue. I ran out to the Colt to put the back seat down, open the hatchback, and insert Jane's custom-made, wooden ramp, so Piggy Sue could make her grand ascension into the back of the vehicle. Before doing so, however, I had the presence of mind to put my books on the floor and cover them with a garbage bag I had in the back (a move I was incredibly thankful for later).

With the *limo* now ready for Her Royal *Swineness*, I stood by the open back like a chauffeur waiting for a dignitary. Soon Jane came out of the house right behind Piggy Sue and began coaxing her to walk down the sidewalk toward the car and ramp. "Come on sweetie," she said, in the same high-pitched voice usually reserved for a baby. And sure enough, Piggy Sue responded and began slowly making her way toward me.

You stupid pig, you better not poop in my car, is all I could think as she began walking up the ramp into the back. Once she was inside, I pulled up the ramp and slid it on its side so it extended between the front seats. Then I closed the trunk and slid behind the wheel while Jane found her way into the passenger seat, the ramp awkwardly between us. As I pulled into the street and began making my way to the kennel, my mind continued to race and for the first time I realized how ridiculous this all would look to anyone observing from the outside; the pig-mobile was on the move!

Once we reached the kennel, the next step was getting Piggy Sue to exit the car and descend the ramp, which was a difficult task for a stubby-legged creature with no spring in its limbs. There was no way she could step up onto the ledge at the back of the car. I thought for sure Jane must have a solution ... but she didn't. I pondered the situation for a moment ... *If I open the passenger door and put the seat forward, maybe I can fit Piggy Sue through the gap between the seat and the door frame. She'll just slide easily through and the problem's solved.* It seemed straightforward enough.

Thinking we had the problem solved, we gave it a shot. I climbed in the back behind Piggy Sue and began to guide her toward the opening. Then I gave her one last gentle nudge, hoping she'd just slide through the gap according to plan. Instead, she became jammed in the hole like a cork in a wine bottle. What followed were the most high-pitched, piercing squeals I've ever heard, coupled with a torrential release of saliva that flowed onto the garbage bag *(thank You, Jesus)* and sprayed other parts of the back seat.

The kennel manager just stood nearby; the expression on his face as if to say, "Don't look at me, this is above my pay grade!"

Running around to the passenger door I reached in, quickly grabbed Piggy Sue under her front legs, and pushed her back into the cargo area. She immediately stopped her squealing and just stood panting. *You stupid pig!* I thought.

Let me interject that, obviously, I didn't have a very Christlike attitude in that moment. *(You think, Ian?)* I agreed to serve an elderly woman at a time of need but when push came to shove, *(literally)*, I was resentful, angry, and didn't display a gracious attitude *(at least on the inside)*.

The lesson: We can't agree to do something and then, when the task becomes difficult, resent the person who asked. No one forced us to go along with it, and we therefore need to look to the Lord for His grace to follow through in a God-honoring manner.

Anyway, back to the story. More determined than ever to get Piggy Sue out of my car, I came up with one last plan. Positioning Jane on one side of the ramp and me on the other, with a burst of anger and adrenaline I grabbed Piggy Sue under her front legs and pulled her up over the ledge. She began walking down the ramp, bouncing back and forth between our shoulders like a ping-pong ball until she finally reached the bottom and stepped off the ramp.

Then, as if on cue, she dropped a load of piggy poop. It was a double relief not only to finally have her out of my vehicle but also to have avoided her little "present."

A week later, after her hospital stay, Jane called to see if I would reprise my role and bring Piggy Sue home. I politely declined— there's only so much fun a man can have in a lifetime!

Why have I told you this story? Was it simply to highlight one of my most bizarre and humorous incidents as a pastor? Well ... yes, it's always fun to tell stories that make me look stupid. However, the true reason is to highlight the importance of accepting the detours in life's journey—the moments when our highway of destiny seemingly diverges from its proper course and begins to take us ... nowhere. In reality, these are often opportunities to serve and bless others and are part of God's plan to further develop our character and teach us to be more Christ-like.

And so, even though it was odd transporting Piggy Sue to the kennel, in the end, it felt good helping Jane in a time of need. First Peter 4:9–10 says, *"Offer hospitality to one another without grumbling. Each one should use whatever gift he has received to serve others, faithfully administering God's grace in its various forms"* (NIV84).

It is clear God wants us to help others with a good attitude, but in the midst of our busy lives, how do any of us know where to serve and who to help, when there are so many needs around us?

That's a question I wrestled with for years. Thankfully, I learned something from Jesus' life that's revolutionizing how I live mine.

In John chapter 5:19, when He was getting heat from the Pharisees for healing a man on the Sabbath (considered work and a violation of the day of rest), Jesus responds by pointing to His Heavenly Father as the instigator of His actions. *"I only do what I see my father doing,"* He says. In other words, "Don't blame Me, guys! I'm just here to obediently do what My Father asks—nothing more nothing less. I healed this man because it was what the Father was doing today. It's as simple as that!"

Have you ever stopped to consider how many people Jesus didn't heal during his three-and-a-half-year ministry? At the Pool of Bethesda (John 5:1–14), where He healed a man of paralysis, there were countless others lying there in much the same condition. Why didn't He heal all of them? What about the time in Mark 1 when Jesus' revival meetings were just heating up in Capernaum? People were being healed and the crowds were getting bigger and bigger. His disciples must have thought they'd hit the jackpot and Jesus' ministry was finally taking off. Maybe they could envision weeks of meetings with ever-increasing followers and huge media coverage throughout the region. Okay, the latter was impossible at the time, but nevertheless, they could sense His notoriety would increase.

After a late night of ministry, however, Jesus still gets up and goes to a quiet place to pray. Two of His disciples eventually go in search of Him and meet Him as He returns from prayer. They inform Him of the crowds and likely want to plan the day. Jesus shocks them, however, when He declares they are to move on to the villages of Galilee where they will be unknown and start the whole process again. I can just imagine the incredulous look on His disciples' faces as they process His request. They might have been thinking such things as, *You mean we're not going to continue ministering here in Capernaum? Things are just getting going. Why would we leave now? There's still so much work to be done!*

Jesus is adamant, however. During His prayer time, it's obvious the Father spoke and revealed the plans for the day; these plans included the villages of Galilee and not Capernaum. Thus, the Son is packing up and moving on in obedience to His Father's wishes. Seems simple enough, but let's consider how challenging it really was to Jesus. First, He had to let people down and not meet their expectations. Second, He had to risk being misunderstood by His very own disciples as it looked like a regressive rather than progressive decision. Yet Jesus was confident in the leading of His Father as obviously, He'd practiced being attentive and cultivating a listening ear.

After hearing a teaching on this passage, I determined to begin developing my own daily practice of listening for the Father's direction. I began writing this question at the top of each journal page: "What are You doing today, Father, and how can I follow You in that?" Then I would take time to quiet myself and listen for any impressions He placed in my mind and heart.

For some of you, this may seem like an odd practice and even a bit scary. "How can I know I'm actually hearing from God?" you may ask. I assure you that over time we can all learn to hear the Lord's "still small voice" (1 Kings 19:12 NKJV) as He prompts us to act. What He shares will never contradict Scripture and will always advance His ultimate purpose of people coming to know and understand His love for them. Asking this question relieves the pressure of trying to figure out how to serve the Father. The onus is on Him to speak and guide us in His purposes; our responsibility is to be open and obedient to His leading.

Soon after starting this journal practice, the Lord answered with an incredible witnessing opportunity. One day, I was heading out to fix something on our minivan. Usually when I have a project, I'm incredibly focused on it to the exclusion of everything else; sadly, at times, even my wife and kids. Yet today, as I purposefully strode out to the van, I suddenly noticed my neighbor Fred (not his real name) walking past and immediately felt compelled to go talk with him. I had a serious discussion with Fred once before but that was a year ago and we had had little connection since. On this day, however, I sensed he was open to another chat.

"Hey Fred," I called as I moved toward the cul de sac. He responded in a friendly manner and we began a casual discussion about the weather and how it was affecting his work as a contractor. Then I said, "How are you doing, Fred? How's it going with your daughters?" I knew Fred was having trouble connecting with his two girls following his divorce with their mother. That question opened a floodgate of emotions as Fred shared his pain and frustration about the situation. As the conversation lengthened he suddenly said, "Can we go sit on your front porch? I've already been out in the sun too much today."

"Absolutely," I said, excited not only about the ongoing discussion but also that Fred was comfortable enough to visit on my home turf. We sat together on the bench in front of our house, and as he poured out his heart, I suddenly heard the Lord's still small voice within my spirit say, *This is what I'm doing today!*

Thank you, Lord, for this opportunity, I thought. *I think I'm finally getting it!* I prayed for Fred at the end of our time together and then he wiped tears from his eyes and said, "I'm so glad we had this time together today. Thank you!"

It was wonderful to encourage and pray for this hurting man, and it gave me a hunger to continue asking the Lord to show me, on a daily basis, where He's working and how I can be involved. The same opportunity is available to all of us if we're open to His leading and then are willing to adjust our schedule to accept His assignment. Keeping this perspective in the forefront of my mind I can ask myself, *When I transported Piggy Sue to the kennel, was that what the Father was doing that day?* I think so, and I also believe He was laughing the whole time!

POINTS TO PONDER

1. How can we cultivate a willing heart and avoid grumbling when we find ourselves inconvenienced by the need to serve others?

2. In what areas does the Lord want you to begin asking Him to guide your steps? In what ways can you practically cultivate a mindset and practice of doing only what you see the Father doing?

3. How can we remain aware of the needs around us and God's leading to meet them, when life's busy and there's so much to do?

PRAYER

"Dear Lord, I thank You that we are Your hands and feet on this earth—that we have the opportunity to serve and help others in Your name. I ask You to help me learn to hear Your voice so that, like Jesus, I will do only what I see You doing. Open my eyes daily to see the opportunities You provide to bless others and lead them closer to You. I ask for Your boldness to move forward in love and to be Your witness. In Jesus' name. Amen."

8

OFF-ROADING:
Navigating the Valleys

As they pass through the Valley of Baca,
they make it a place of springs;
the autumn rains also cover it with pools.
Psalm 84:6 (NIV84)

M Y CONFLICTED EMOTIONS SWIRLED WITHIN ME AS I SAT IN the conference and tried focusing on the guest speakers and those leading us in singing and worship to God. On the one hand, I was excited about the prospect of leaving Medicine Hat and starting a new church in Calgary. On the other, I was pained at the prospect of pulling up stakes and leaving the city we'd called home for nearly nine years—the place we'd raised our four sons and developed strong, enduring friendships both in our church and in the community at large. It was a tug of war between the comfort and safety of the familiar and the challenge and adventure of the unknown.

I was attending *The Pursuit* conference in Medicine Hat, Alberta—an annual event hosted by my good friend Antonio Baldovinos—and I was struggling to stay focused. However, as Christian recording artist Jason Upton began sharing between songs, I snapped out of my fog as I realized how relevant his story was to my situation. Jason shared how he had heard the Lord speaking to him at a very pivotal moment in his music career. He was comfortable and successful and could picture himself on a mountaintop of achievement where he was celebrated, recognized, and treated with great favor and respect by others. Even at this pinnacle moment, it was as if he could envision God pointing to another, much higher peak some distance away.

As Jason spoke, I could imagine the distant snowcapped mountain with jagged peaks reaching high into the heavens just like the majestic Rockies near Calgary, Alberta. The view from that towering height would be much more awe-inspiring, breathtaking, and expansive, than the vista from the smaller mountain.

In his vision, the Lord then said to Jason, "How would you like to go to that higher place in your worship ministry?"

Jason's answer was an emphatic "yes," but then he began to think of the logistics of making the trip. He asked God, "How will we get there?" The Lord then pointed to the long, deep valley between the two mountains. Jason would have to descend from his current summit, walk through the lowlands below, and then scale the side of the much taller mountain. He would move from prominence to hiddenness, and finally to a higher level of prominence again. There was risk involved and the journey wouldn't be easy.

Sensing Jason's hesitation the Lord said to him, *"Aw come on Jace, it'll be fun. And then in three to five years you'll be over there,"* as if pointing to the much higher peak.

Tears began filling my eyes as I listened to Jason's story. I could sense the Holy Spirit making the parallel with my situation. I had thoroughly enjoyed my nearly ten years ministering in Medicine Hat. My work as Senior Pastor at The Bridge and time as President of the Medicine Hat Evangelical Association (twenty plus churches working together to minister to the city) were very rewarding and fulfilling. I had profile and many friends. There's no way I'd leave that if it weren't for the encouragement of others and the call of God on our lives.

To obey that call, however, meant leaving the comfortable,

secure pinnacle of my current success, and descending into the shadows of the valley below—uncertain who would join us in the church plant, where we would meet, and how God would accomplish this great dream. As Jason said "three to five years," I somehow sensed that was the time frame when I, too, would move to a much higher level of ministry effectiveness—if I obeyed now, stepped off the mountain and began moving through the valley. It's as if I could hear the Lord saying to me, *"Aw, come on E, it'll be fun!"*

That night I left the meeting with a picture of where I was going and what it would take to get there. As John Maxwell has written, "You have to give up to go up."[1] This principle is highlighted in the passage from Psalm 84:7, *"they go from strength to strength, till each appears before God in Zion."* If you're like me, you'd prefer life be a series of strong and successful moments—a constant upward progression with no low points in between. This Psalm, however, describes a journey where we must sometimes pass through dry, hot lowlands before rising to the new level of God's blessing and provision—off-roading, as it were, that creates new highways, taking us to even greater heights with astounding viewpoints we could not have experienced had we stayed on the main road.

Verse six of this psalm says: *"As they pass through the Valley of Baca, they make it a place of springs; the autumn rains also cover it with pools."* Baca means "weeping" in Hebrew; *Valley of Baca,* therefore, means "Valley of Weeping"—a specific geographical location pilgrims had to pass through on their way to worship God on Mount Zion in Jerusalem.

Faussett's Bible Dictionary further adds to the explanation and paints a stark picture indeed: "Baca is the Arabic for a balsam-like shrub with round large fruit, from which if a leaf be plucked a tear-like drop exudes. As the valley of Baca represents a valley of spiritual drought where the only water is that of "tears," so the pilgrim's "making it a well" (by having "his strength in Jehovah") symbolizes continuous comfort and salvation."[2]

With this in mind, imagine a dry, desolate valley where the

only vegetation is a balsam-like shrub and the only moisture to be found is the tear-like drop of water released when a leaf is removed from that plant. This makes for a rather depressing picture, and yet how many times does our spiritual journey resemble that image: a place where we haven't heard from God in a while, our physical circumstances seem hopeless, and the only moisture is that of our tears.

It would be easy to dismiss this as unnecessary and unspiritual if not for the fact it's a part of the journey to glory outlined in Psalm 84. To finish the course, have God's highways built in our heart, and arrive in Heaven, we must travel through the Valley of Baca. These tearful moments are necessary for our character development and are important for the advancement of God's purposes in and through us.

We need only look at some Old Testament examples to see the truth of this. Moses and David both spent time in the desert prior to their promotions. Joseph languished in a figurative desert of service to Potiphar and later as manager of a dank Egyptian jail. Those desert experiences were a humbling and breaking process for these men of God. Moses entered the desert a refugee from Pharaoh's court—educated and accomplished in all the ways of Egypt; he left the desert as a humble shepherd, now called to lead an entire nation by God's grace. David entered the desert as a fugitive of King Saul and spent years fleeing through the wasteland with his band of Mighty Men; he left the desert and became king of an entire nation. Joseph was taken from his family and transported through the desert to Egypt where he served in Potiphar's house and later in prison; he left his "desert" of service to become the leader of Egypt—second only to Pharaoh.

Of course, our greatest example is always Jesus himself. Matthew 4 describes His desert experience. Hungry and weak after fasting forty days and nights, Jesus is tempted by the devil three times—on each occasion declaring and brandishing Scripture like a weapon to overcome intense pressure to compromise His mission.

Interestingly, Jesus' time of trial immediately follows His greatest ministry moment to date. In Matthew 3, He travels from Galilee to the Jordan to be baptized, very appropriately, by His cousin John the Baptist. As soon as Jesus is baptized and He comes up out of the water, Heaven is opened, and He sees the Spirit of God descending on Him like a dove. Then God the Father calls from Heaven (I imagine it was a loud, booming voice that startled everyone present) and declares *"This is my Son, whom I love; with him I am well pleased"* (Matthew 3:16). Wow! What a euphoric, exhilarating experience for Jesus! Heaven opens, the Holy Spirit descends on Him, and His Father openly affirms His loving approval before many witnesses. What a mountaintop! It doesn't get much better!

However, Matthew 4:1 (NIV84) immediately describes His descent into the *valley*: *"Then Jesus was led by the Spirit into the desert to be tempted by the devil."* Talk about being dropped on your head! The contrast of experiences couldn't have been greater for Jesus, and in His humanity, I'm sure He acutely felt the painful isolation along with the physical stress of fasting. After His season of trial and temptation was over, however, "Jesus returned to Galilee in the power of the Spirit, and news about him spread through the whole countryside. He was teaching in their synagogues, and everyone praised him" (Luke 4:14–15).

Jesus' ascent from His *Baca Valley* certainly took Him beyond the pinnacle of His baptism experience. Empowered like never before, everyone took notice. From limited exposure before a band of people standing at the Jordan, *"news about him spread through the whole countryside."* He went from mountaintop to valley, to higher summit still—in other words, "from strength to strength."

The desert experiences of life are vital if we're to completely fulfill God's calling and purposes for our lives. In the desert, something is produced which God can take and supernaturally empower for His service and destiny. Therefore, how do we make sure we pass through those *Baca valleys* in a manner honoring God instead of them becoming our own personal *Death Valley* of vision, confidence, and success?

First of all, we need to realize such moments are only temporary and not indicative of what will happen the rest of our lives. Tough times are not the occasion to lapse into self-pity, curl up in a ball, and die.

Secondly, we need to make the decision this desert experience is going to make us better rather than bitter. When my wife experienced a grievous family tragedy at the age of nineteen, she had a key decision to make. Would she allow that terrible tragedy to affect her view of God and then lapse into a state of bitterness and despair? Or, even though she didn't know why this had happened, would she still choose to believe in God's goodness and that He would fulfill His purposes for her and her brother and sisters? Thankfully she chose the latter and is as much in love with Jesus as ever and is pursuing the Lord's ever-expanding call upon her life.

Thirdly, as we pass through the Valley of Baca, we must make sure we don't live in a state of regret about both past successes and failures. Paul the Apostle had plenty of reasons to look back at incredible achievements and moments of abysmal personal failure. As a student of the great Jewish teacher Gamaliel, Paul became one of the strictest adherents to the Pharisaic religious sect and was one of the rising stars in Judaism. Because of his rigid beliefs, he zealously persecuted the early Christians, witnessed the stoning of Stephen in Jerusalem, and then set off for Damascus to arrest the Christians there. It was on this journey he encountered Christ. As an apostle, therefore, Paul had occasion to recall his popularity as a "Pharisee of Pharisees" (Acts 23:6) and to replay his involvement in Stephen's stoning and the persecution of the church. Dwelling on either extreme would hinder him from fully pursuing his destiny and fulfilling God's plans. Recognizing this, Paul determined to do "one thing"—forget what was behind and strain toward God's future purposes for his life (Philippians 3:13). In Romans 8:28 he writes: *"And we know that in all things God works for the good of those who love him, who have been called according to his purpose."* The Bible is clear both good and bad circumstances are used by the Lord to fulfill His purposes in our lives. He can redeem all things for His glory if we keep a right heart and attitude.

Finally, we need to realize the Lord is always with us even when we're passing through the hot, dry Valley of Baca and don't sense even a hint of His presence. Just before ascending into Heaven, Jesus encouraged His disciples with these words: *"And surely I am with you always, to the very end of the age"* (Matthew 28:20b). Jesus was telling them, "I know the task I'm giving you isn't easy, but I promise I'll always be with you—even when circumstances seem contrary and you don't really feel My presence." Two thousand years later, Jesus' promise is still true. Even when He asks us to leave our comfort zone and descend into a *baca valley*, He'll always be with us and we may even hear Him say, "Aw, come on, . . . it'll be fun!"

POINTS TO PONDER

1. Are there any *mountaintop*s of success from which the Lord is asking you to descend so you can eventually be much more fruitful in the future?

2. Are you determined to continue moving through your current valley or have you stalled out and lapsed into discouragement or self-pity?

3. Have you made the decision in life's difficulties to become *better* rather than *bitter*? Is there any such bitterness in your heart from past situations from which you need to repent, so you can move forward again in God's purposes?

4. Are you living in a state of regret regarding past successes or failures, or have you turned your attention toward the next *mountainto*p God has in store?

5. In spite of your feelings and spiritual dryness, will you recognize the Lord is still with you and committed to helping you fulfill His purposes for your life?

PRAYER

Here's a sample prayer that may help you express some of these thoughts to the Lord:

"Dear Lord, You know I've been in a Baca valley lately—hot, dry and feeling separated from Your presence. Please forgive me where I've allowed bitterness to creep in—even causing me to doubt Your goodness and love for me. I no longer want to live in regret regarding the past but choose now, with the help and power of Your Holy Spirit, to put those things behind me and begin moving ahead with renewed strength and positive expectation about Your plans for my future. I thank You for always being with me. In Jesus' name, Amen."

9

THE HIGHWAY OF TEARS:
Comforting Others

M Y MIND RACED AS I CONSIDERED THE SITUATION. *WHAT has happened? Is it as serious as it sounds?* Moments earlier I'd received a call urging me to immediately pick up my girlfriend Val from work and take her to her grandmother's house. No details were given that would lessen the anxiety and remove the knot from the pit of my stomach. Driving in the car, Val and I laughed nervously as we considered what could await us. We said a quick prayer for Gramma, assuming we were being called to her home because of a sudden health emergency.

Arriving at the house, we sprinted across the road, up the steps, and through the front door. Confusion and uncertainty washed over us as, surprisingly, we saw Gramma standing at the top of the first-floor landing, steady, composed, healthy. Questioningly we glanced around the house noting the aunts and uncles huddled together at the kitchen table, eyes red, cheeks stained with tears—Val's mother and father, Allen and Katie Greeno, conspicuously absent. Before a word was spoken, Val intuitively understood the tragedy at hand, cried out in disbelief, and then ran to her Gramma's room, threw herself on the bed, and wept. As I stood in numbed shock, Gramma confirmed our worst fears. "Allen and Katie were killed in a car accident today," she said in a sad whisper.

Ironically, that morning Val's parents had been on their way to visit a man who'd recently lost his wife in a traffic collision—a caring gesture not uncommon for the down-to-earth farming couple who always had room at the table for one more guest. About an hour down the road they had rounded a sharp curve in the highway and collided with another vehicle that had lost control on black ice. In an instant, my 19-year-old girlfriend's parents were in Eternity and our lives, and that of her three younger siblings, Les (17), Sherry (15), and Doreen (13), would never be the same.

The days following were a blur of funeral preparations, visits with friends and relatives, and restless nights with strange dreams as our minds and spirits tried to reconcile with the unthinkable.

The funeral was a mix of quiet grieving and brave celebration as one speaker after another praised the great love and care shown by Val's parents. The twelve hundred mourners for the humble farming couple were befitting a civic dignitary and reflected the incredible impact of their lives.

That morning, Val awoke, sensing God wanted her to speak at the funeral and challenge those in attendance to serve Him and live in a manner honoring of her parents' spiritual legacy. And therefore, in the midst of her intense grief and sorrow, the brave young lady climbed the podium, took a deep breath, and with a strong voice encouraged everyone to live for the Lord. "Don't let them die in vain!" she implored as she recounted how her parents had prayed for many in attendance to eventually become Christ followers.

The next day the local paper carried the story on the front page with an inset picture of Val giving her address—an amazing testament of God's grace and strength in a time of tragedy and death. Our life highway had suddenly descended into a deep "Valley of Weeping," but it was both encouraging and inspiring to see my girlfriend "make it a place of springs" for others by obeying the Lord's prompting and sharing her faith.

I married Val ten months later at the ripe old age of 21. Factoring in my father's death from cancer when I was 12, the two of us had already known much loss and tragedy during our relatively short lives. Those first years saw either one or the other of her sisters live with us for extended periods of time (something we considered a great privilege, but which also had its challenging moments). We grew up quickly, but God, our relatives, and our church family were always there for Val and me during the difficult times. They stood with us as we engaged in the vital process of healing, which has no shortcuts and is necessary if we're to move on with our lives after a "Baca Valley" in our life journey.

I've gained much wisdom through the different valley seasons of life. These valleys often leave us in a state of emotional (if not spiritual or physical) turmoil. While it's normal to mourn, the key is embracing the healing journey so we can move through the valley and not become stuck emotionally or spiritually. I believe the first step to healing is understanding there's a grieving process common to us all.

In 1969, psychiatrist Elisabeth Kubler-Ross introduced what has become known as the *five stages of grief*, based upon studies of patients facing terminal illness. Over time, however, the principles have also been applied to other types of negative life changes or losses such as the death of a loved one or relational breakup.[1]

These stages are:

1. **Denial** – "This can't be happening to me."

2. **Anger** – "Why is this happening? Who is to blame?"

3. **Bargaining** – "Make this not happen, and in return, I will _____"

4. **Depression** – "I'm too sad to do anything."

5. **Acceptance** – "I'm at peace with what happened."

In hindsight, I can see how our family moved through these stages after the loss of Val's parents. At first, we all had a measure of denial and couldn't fully comprehend that something so tragic had happened. Upon receiving the news from our pastor, John Syratt,

Val's 13-year old sister Doreen screamed, "You're lying," and broke down in tears. Val cried out "No, no," as she ran into her grandma's bedroom and threw herself on the bed in despair. My denial was more muted as my whole body tingled in shock and I mumbled, "Oh God, Oh God," as I tried to comprehend the situation.

Just over a year after her parents' death, Val also experienced a time of severe depression. This led her to jump in the car and leave me on three different occasions—striving to run away from her pain. Thankfully, she only had a 1980 four-cylinder Dodge Omni and couldn't get over the mountain passes as she attempted to get to Vancouver, British Columbia. Instead, she turned around and came home, saving me from great anxiety in those pre-cellphone days.

Knowing these are the usual responses and that a person heals with time should encourage everyone encountering a Baca "Valley of Weeping" experience. It's also helpful to know grief is very personal. As Smith, Robinson, and Segal write in their article Coping with Loss, "Contrary to popular belief, you do not have to go through each stage in order to heal. In fact, some people resolve their grief without going through any of these stages. And if you do go through these stages of grief, you probably won't experience them in a neat, sequential order, so don't worry about what you "should" be feeling or which stage you're supposed to be in."[2] These experts support what Val and I were told at the time; there are no rules to the grieving process because it's a journey unique to each person.

Looking back at our experience, I believe there were two primary keys that helped us deal with our grief and come to a place of healing. The **first key** was to **gain the encouragement and assistance of others**, an action confirmed by the authors in this same article:

"The single most important factor in healing from loss is having the support of other people. Even if you aren't comfortable talking about your feelings under normal circumstances, it's important to express them when you are grieving. Sharing your loss makes the burden of grief easier to carry. Wherever the support comes from, accept it and do not grieve alone. Connecting to others will help you heal."[3]

For Val and me, our support came primarily from our church family at New Hope Christian Centre in Lethbridge, Alberta. Pastor John Syratt and his wife Leith, along with the other "New Hopers," provided both practical and emotional assistance to us all. In particular, I remember how fellow church member and good friend Mike Bollinger came to support me at just the right time. Because I wasn't yet married to Val and therefore not officially part of the family, I found myself in a type of relational no man's land. She and her siblings mourned together at their farm with many visits from friends and family, while for the most part, I remained alone in the city. Val was rightly consumed with concern for her family and the pain of her loss, which naturally created some distance between us. I wanted to be respectful and give her space, but that also meant I became isolated. Several days after Allen and Katie's death and a few days before the funeral, I sat alone in my mother's basement suite feeling sad, lost, and confused. The isolation just added to my pain and I felt like no one cared. Suddenly, the ringing of the phone jarred me out of my self-pitied stupor.

"Hey, how are you doin'?" asked Mike on the other end of the line.

"Well, I've been better," I said as I felt a lump in my throat and tears welling up in my eyes.

"I'm coming over," he said quickly before I could respond.

"Sounds good," I mumbled before hanging up.

Ten minutes later there was a knock on my door. I opened it to find my 6 foot 5 friend standing there with a small peanut puppet on his finger, reminiscent of the Planter's character without the top hat.

"Hi," Mike said in a high-pitched voice as he moved the puppet. "Be polite," Mike said sternly to the peanut, who then responded, "Hi, please."

Such a ridiculous moment, but one I will never forget. That goofy peanut act broke the tension and I laughed and laughed. Later, Mike and I took a drive around the city lake and he poured life into me on one of the darkest January nights I can recall.

Along with the support of friends, we can also gain strength from joining a grief support group or talking to a therapist or counselor. The bottom line is that we *not* walk the journey alone.

The **second key** to dealing with our grief was learning to properly **take care of ourselves** during that stressful time. As Smith, Robinson, and Segal write, "The stress of a major loss can quickly deplete your energy and emotional reserves. Looking after your physical and emotional needs will help you get through this difficult time."[4]

Here are a few suggestions they make in the article about how to practice this self-care:

1. Face Your Feelings; "In order to heal, you have to acknowledge the pain." Avoidance only prolongs the grieving process and can lead to difficulties like depression, anxiety, substance abuse, and health problems.

2. Look after your physical health; since body, soul, and spirit are connected, when you feel good physically you also feel better emotionally. Getting enough sleep, eating right, and exercising are all helpful practices.

3. Don't let anyone, including yourself, tell you how to feel; since everyone responds to grief differently. It's okay to be angry, cry or not cry, or even laugh and have moments of joy.

Sometimes others don't understand the range of emotions you're experiencing. When my dad died of cancer, I was out of school the week prior to his death as I made trips to and from the hospital and our family stayed with friends in Calgary. (I lived about forty miles away in a small community.) It was an emotionally draining time as I said "goodbye" to him and braced myself for his passing. Once he was gone I then had to spend time with visiting family members (all of whom were much older than me) as we prepared for the celebration of his life. By the day of the memorial service, I was greatly looking forward to seeing some of my friends again. I vividly recall feeling great joy as I met them in the church parking lot prior to the service. When I finally returned to school, however, one of my friends said another classmate, who attended the memorial, was very surprised at my joyful exuberance and questioned why I wouldn't show more grief at the loss of my dad. The comment hurt because I deeply loved my dad and had shed many tears. However, by the time of the service, the joy of seeing my peers eclipsed even that grief.

Moral of the story: We don't know the whole picture and should always be careful about judging other's actions as they grieve.

4. Plan ahead for grief triggers. Anniversaries, birthdays and other milestones can reawaken memories and feelings about a loved one. Be prepared for an "emotional wallop"—which is normal—and plan accordingly.

I'll never forget the first Christmas Eve after Val's parents died. The five of us, (Val and I, and her three siblings) sat quietly in the soft glow of the Christmas tree lights as memories of Christmases past made Allen and Katie's absence seem unbearable. Thankfully, God gave us His grace and strength during all those "firsts;" the pain gradually fading each succeeding year as time passed and He healed our hearts.

Eventually, our family became a conduit of God's comfort to others. Today we're deeply touched when tragedy strikes a family and someone suddenly dies. Because of our past, we're filled with deep compassion and can pray for them from a place of understanding. In 2 Corinthians 1:3–5, Paul the Apostle writes, *"Praise be to the God and Father of our Lord Jesus Christ, the Father of compassion and the God of all comfort, who comforts us in all our troubles, so that we can comfort those in any trouble with the comfort we ourselves have received from God. For just as the sufferings of Christ flow over into our lives, so also through Christ our comfort overflows"* (NIV84).

Paul knew about troubles, suffering, and distress. He endured beatings, shipwrecks, and imprisonment and paid a high price for the advance of the gospel. Reflecting upon these difficulties, however, he saw them in a greater light. He realized the comfort the Lord gave him in those tough times could be transferred to others in their similar trials. It was as if Paul understood every difficulty produced a wellspring of comfort within him that could refresh those in need. The word *comfort* in this passage is *"paraclesis"* in Greek and communicates the idea of one person standing alongside another to encourage and support his friend. It's also the same word describing the Holy Spirit (*Paraclete*) who strengthens and guides us.[5]

We must realize our difficult experiences are never just about us but can provide the background and grace to stand alongside others as an encouragement, support, and strength. Knowing this helps us see our valley times from a different perspective. By God's grace, we choose to make life's deserts a place of springs (Psalm 84:6), with these moments becoming God's tool (source) to add strength, stability, and refreshment to others—a testimony to build them up in their times of need.

Referring to followers of Christ, Revelations 12:11 (NIV84) says, *"They overcame him* (the devil) *by the blood of the Lamb and by the word of their testimony..."* Jesus' death on the cross paid the price for our sins and gave us victory over the devil, but this verse also reveals that declaring what God has done in our lives is a powerful way to defeat darkness. It's time to unleash this secret weapon and effectively use our testimonies of God's grace to release comfort into others. Our reluctance to share is sometimes because we're uncertain how to share such a story.

Here are some helpful thoughts:

Before – Describe the difficulty you were in before you experienced the Lord's comfort and touch in your life. This should be specific yet brief. If you are sharing how you came to know Jesus Christ in a personal way, give a general overview of your former lifestyle and the desperate needs in your life before meeting Christ.

How – Next, share how the Lord comforted you. How were your deepest needs met? What were the circumstances surrounding this life-changing moment? If you are sharing your salvation testimony, provide the details of how you came to know Jesus.

After – Finally, share tangibly the effects God's comfort has had on your life. What has changed? How have you helped others because of your experience? Your salvation testimony will show how the problems of your former lifestyle are solved by your relationship with Christ.[6]

Hopefully, after sharing your experiences, you'll have occasion to pray and minister so the other person can receive God's comfort. The most exciting facet is leading others to Christ so they also have the joy of knowing Him as their Savior. (Please see Chapter 19 for how to embark on this relationship.)

Sharing our testimonies illustrates the Lord's power to transform lives. I like to say, "Nothing is ever wasted with God." He takes every situation, and if we let Him, uses it for His glory. Romans 8:28 gives evidence of this point: *"And we know that in all things God works for the good of those who love him, who have been called according to his purpose."*

In their book "Live Your Passion, Tell Your Story, Change Your World," Bob Reccord and Randy Singer challenge us to use our experiences to reach those in our everyday lives. They write,

". . . Jesus spent most of his time not inside the temple, but out where the people were in life's daily tasks. And he taught those who followed him to do the same . . . So he transformed tax collectors, commercial fishermen, political activists, and a host of marketplace people. Besides, who could reach others in the marketplace of life better than those who knew it well from personal experience?"[7]

Just as God comforted and healed our family, led us through the stages of grief, and turned our tragedy into a testimony of comfort, I pray He will do the same in the dark valleys of your life. May each of us become a catalyst for transformation in the lives of others as we allow God's comfort to fill and flow through us!

POINTS TO PONDER

1. In what areas has the Lord comforted you? How can you become a source of comfort to others in this same area?

2. Is there any grief in your life you continue hanging on to rather than embracing God's comfort?

3. Are you walking through any of the grief stages? How can you allow the Lord to heal you?

4. Who needs to hear a testimony of God's grace in your life? (Begin to pray and ask the Lord to provide opportunities to share.)

5. Based upon the simple three-point outline (as previously suggested) what would your testimony look like?

PRAYER

"Father, I thank You for the ways You have comforted me throughout my life. In the difficult and challenging moments, You have never left me alone but have always stood beside me providing encouragement and strength. Lord, as You have touched my life I now ask You to draw upon that wellspring of comfort within me so others can likewise be encouraged and strengthened in their times of trial. I thank You that nothing is ever wasted with You because You can even redeem my weaknesses and failures to bring comfort to others. I look forward to what You will accomplish and I will be careful to give all glory and praise to You. In Jesus' name, Amen."

10

DESERT STORM:
Persevering in the Call

I JUMPED IN THE CAR, THREW THE GEAR SHIFT INTO REVERSE, and bolted out of the driveway. *I'm going to give them a piece of my mind,* I thought as I accelerated down the road. *I've had it with this two-bit town. My time here has been nothing but loss and despair, and now this added disappointment. I'm out of here!*

It was October 1996 and my mother had just passed away from pneumonia after a series of strokes and declining health. Just the day before I had said my goodbyes, and as she gasped for air while on a ventilator, I said to my mother, "Just go home to be with Jesus"—and she did. Grieving her loss, I had just received other discouraging news. I was already on the verge of leaving Taber, Alberta, but this new development made me feel like I'd reached the tipping point and it was definitely time to go.

There are times when we're right in the middle of such a "desert" or Baca season and there's no relief in sight. On every side, we see shimmering waves of intense heat bouncing off the white, sunbaked sand of our lives, blurring our view and sometimes creating a mirage of distant refreshment. The oasis is always false, however, and all we find is more white-hot sand and an ever-increasing thirst for "water" to satisfy our parched souls. Desperate for relief, the temptation is to flee somewhere—anywhere—that might provide some shade and cool refreshment.

This particular Baca season had begun nearly a year before, in November 1995, when I purchased a franchise for publishing a free television listings magazine. Advertising sales were to cover the cost of publication and consumers, in turn, would be thrilled at having a free TV magazine and would therefore support the advertisers. I would eventually rake in huge profits, build a successful organization, and have lots of time to serve my local church and follow God's purposes for my life. This magazine concept thrived in other parts of Canada and the United States, so I was confident it would take off in Southern Alberta.

Was I wrong!

Selling for the new publication began in earnest in January 1996. It was a particularly cold and snowy stretch of winter and retailers were in their post-Christmas advertising mode; they weren't buying. I spent many a day listening to the crisp, crunching sound of snow beneath my steps as I trudged from business to business without success. All I had were a few samples of the TV Facts magazine from other franchises, a rate card, and a lot of optimism about what my publication could accomplish in Lethbridge, Alberta.

It wasn't enough, however, and except for a few brave souls, the response was much the same everywhere: "We like the concept but are unwilling to invest until we see your magazine in print and can gauge its success." I would always smile, shake the person's hand, and promise to return once we published, but the thought consistently in my mind was, *How will I ever get published if you aren't willing to take the initial risk of supporting me?* It was a very serious catch-22.

Days turned into weeks, and weeks turned into months (three to be precise), which was longer than most other franchisees spent getting their magazines off the ground. As time dragged on, I watched our savings plummet. My carefully calculated business plan was out the window as my resources and confidence drained. Every day it became harder and harder to get out of bed, climb into my cold, frosty car, make the half-hour trek to Lethbridge, and then begin eight hours of seemingly futile cold calling (both figuratively and literally). There were a few sales here and there, but I was still considerably short of the advertising revenue needed to begin publishing.

Fear and panic began filling my soul as I thought of Val and our then three small children (Lyndon still just a twinkle) at home depending solely on me to provide while our limited savings continued to fall. *I spent $25,000 for this franchise and if I can't get it off the ground it will be worthless,* I thought. *Why did I make such a foolish decision? We prayed, planned, sought counsel, and agreed it was God's will, but now everything's falling apart! How could I be so wrong? What if I fail? I could never handle such failure! I'd be marked for life!*

Such thoughts swirled around my head and my emotional and spiritual state began to mirror the wintry, blizzard conditions outside. I became confused and cried easily because of the pressure. It felt like I was at the edge of a cliff staring at an abyss of weakness and failure. I was at the end of my ability and knew it. I always worked so hard to be in control and for most of my life had succeeded in everything I'd done. Not this time. My best efforts were producing little results and time was running out.

In desperation, I cried out to God; "Lord, please help me. I'm at the end of myself and can't continue without Your intervention." He answered my prayer. Along with the encouragement of friends and family, He led me to seek medical advice and our doctor prescribed some medication which helped even out my emotions and restore balance to my system. As a result, I regained emotional strength and finally began making traction in sales, taking Val along with me for moral support as I made the last push to achieve my revenue goal and publish. Overall, starting the magazine felt like a birthing process and the last few pushes were indeed the hardest.

Finally, I was there. Enough ads were sold to begin producing

TV Facts of Greater Lethbridge. What relief I felt as I planned my first edition and created my inaugural ads.

However, just as my business was finally getting off the ground, my involvement in our local church was about to be grounded for a while. Val and I were leaders of one of the weekly house groups where people met to study the Bible, pray, and enjoy each other's company amid the steady grind of life. We were also on the leadership team, and in spite of our recent struggles, our positions provided some solace because at least, we were fulfilling the original purpose for us moving to Taber. Our trials and challenges were worth it if we were helping advance the purposes of New Life Church.

Ultimately, however, the stress and pressure of getting the TV magazine to the point of being published took too high a toll and we ended up relinquishing these church leadership roles just as magazine distribution began. The sting of these leadership setbacks remained for some time, but in the back of my mind, I held out hope I would eventually be in a position where I could regain leadership of our house group (and perhaps also a seat on the leadership team of the church).

As the months passed from winter to spring and then spring to summer, the publishing of my magazine saw many revenue highs and lows as I sought to develop a consistent advertising base. As we entered fall, sales were beginning to slip significantly and I was making very little money on each edition. As a result, when my mom passed away the first of October, I was again experiencing great financial pressure and her death further increased my stress and pain. This was immediately followed by the news that our former house group would have new leaders, but it wouldn't be us! Some good friends of ours were being tapped to take it over. The timing of the announcement was no one's fault, but it was the final straw for a soul already grieving and suffering the pain of great loss.

That's when I jumped in the car to visit Pastor Doug and Karen Shimoda and talk to them about their decision. Arriving at their home, I rang the doorbell and waited impatiently for them to answer. Months of frustration was ready to spill out of my mouth and I'm sure Doug could tell that from the look on my face. They invited me into the family room and I began talking almost immediately after sitting down on the couch.

"I just heard today you're changing the leadership of our old house group. Why didn't you give it back to Val and me? We're ready, we can do it," I stammered, trying to hold back tears. "Why wouldn't you consider us? I've always held out hope we might get it back some time, but now this!"

To their credit, Doug and Karen were very gracious about my outburst and sought to encourage me and explain their decision. After our discussion, they prayed and asked God to provide comfort during my time of loss, both in the death of my mother and the areas of ministry. I appreciated their genuine empathy and compassion but left their home recognizing I still had a lot of unresolved disappointment and anger.

The next week was a blur of preparations for my mother's funeral, the hosting of friends and family, the service itself, and finally some downtime to recuperate. After the dust settled, I evaluated our situation and decided it was time to move back to Lethbridge—a city thirty minutes west of us that we had left nearly two years earlier. The TV magazine was based there and my disabled brother Peter was a resident. With my mother's death, I reasoned I should live closer so I could provide greater support to him. Plus, it seemed like there was nothing happening on the church front anymore and we wouldn't be missed in Taber anyway.

Logically, everything pointed to us moving back to Lethbridge and writing the whole Taber experience off as a terrible experiment. I shared my thoughts with Val and the rationale made sense to her as well. Immediately we began checking rental advertisements in *The Lethbridge Herald* and found a suitable duplex in the northern part of the city. We arranged for a viewing and a couple of days later met to tour the home. I was already in the city, so Val and the boys made the trip from Taber on their own.

The duplex was clean, well maintained, and had enough rooms for our family of five. The price was also right, so we agreed we would rent and immediately wrote our deposit check. We then headed back to Taber, Val and the boys in our van and me in the car.

Driving home in the darkness, I felt uneasy about the decision. *Are we sure this is what God wants us to do?* I wondered. *Moving back to Lethbridge is a big step, and even though it's perfectly logical, is it really the Lord's best for us?*

After mulling over these thoughts during the thirty-minute drive, I arrived home with my wife and kids pulling up in the van a few minutes later. As Val entered the house I could tell she was troubled. "What's wrong?" I asked, noticing her red eyes and tear-stained cheeks.

"I cried all the way home from Lethbridge," she said. "I feel like God's telling me if we leave Taber we'll forfeit the plans He has for us. I sense His grief over our decision to move."

I nodded as she spoke and said, "I feel uneasy too, like we're about to step out of God's will for our lives. We better cancel the duplex rental. I just hope the landlord will release us from the lease and give us back our deposit."

Thankfully, the man was gracious to us and said he'd tear up the check immediately. We breathed a huge sigh of relief and felt peace re-enter our souls. Our situation in Taber was still the same, but we knew it was better to endure tough circumstances in the will of God than to run without His blessing.

It would be four more years of struggling to make a living while commuting to and from Lethbridge before the call came to move to Medicine Hat and lead the church there. However, it was also four years of obeying the last order we'd received from God—to move to Taber and serve the church there. That obedience brought the blessing of His peace in the midst of storms, the development of tremendous friendships, and an eventual release and blessing from our pastors to lead our own church. In the short term, we became the volunteer youth leaders and enjoyed three fruitful years in that role.

What did we learn from that season? That when your life highway seems to wind aimlessly between God's promise (the call), and its fulfillment (the appointment), you continue to follow that path no matter what—you never leave an assignment God has given you until He releases you to move on. We can abort God's plans for our lives if we make comfort such an idol that we choose to run from pressure and difficulty in order to escape our desert seasons. My time in Taber was just such a transition period and I often wonder how many Christians flee prematurely and miss out on future blessing.

A powerful Bible passage about this is found in the book of Hebrews. The writer is encouraging persecuted Jewish Christians to not turn back to Judaism in light of the pressure they're experiencing. He exhorts them to keep doing what God has called them to do—no matter what! He writes,

> *So do not throw away your confidence; it will be richly rewarded. You need to persevere so that when you have done the will of God, you will receive what he has promised. For, "In just a little while, he who is coming will come and will not delay." And, "But my righteous one will live by faith. And I take no pleasure in the one who shrinks back." But we do not belong to those who shrink back and are destroyed, but to those who have faith and are saved"* (Hebrews 10:35–39 NIV).

In the end, our confidence in God was, indeed, rewarded. As Val and I persevered in Taber and followed God's will, He was working to fulfill His promises to us. Ultimately, we were promoted to a leadership assignment that had been in our hearts all along. For Val and me it was important we remained confident God would complete what He had started.

This confident perseverance through the no man's land between God's promise (the call) and its fulfillment (the appointment) is true faith: "confidence in what we hope for and assurance about what we do not see" (Hebrews 11:1). Hebrews 11 goes on to highlight the heroes who showcased such faith and confidence, including: Noah, who received God's call to build a life-saving vessel and then persevered for 120 years before the ark was completed and the promised flood came (v.7); Abraham, who God called to migrate to a land that would eventually be His inheritance, even though he didn't fully know where he was going (vv. 8–9). Ultimately, it would be about 540 years until the Israelites entered that Promised Land.[1] Abraham's wife Sarah, who, despite being past her time of childbearing, waited twenty-five years from when God initially promised an heir to when she miraculously held little Isaac in her arms (Hebrews 11:11–12).

Following this "Hall of Faith," we're immediately encouraged in Hebrews 12:1 to let their incredible trust in God inspire us to *"throw off everything that hinders and the sin that so easily entangles. And let us run with perseverance the race marked out for us,"*— that is, continue steadfastly on the specific journey and highway He's called us to.

The author of Hebrews then highlights Jesus as our ultimate example, *"the pioneer and perfecter"* of our faith who *"For the joy set before him … endured the cross, scorning its shame, and sat down at the right hand of the throne of God"* (Hebrews 12:2). He perfectly modeled the life of faith. When we're tempted to give up or quit, we need to follow this admonition in vs. 3, *"Consider him who endured such opposition from sinners, so that you will not grow weary and lose heart."*

I find it interesting the call to die an excruciating death on the cross was like an act of joy to Jesus. He sees the pain and suffering, but even more so, He sees the joy of fulfilling His Father's will and providing liberation from sin for all mankind.

Likewise, we need to ask God to help us envision the joyful

results that will be produced by our obedience and willingness to persevere in our call. In fact, Scripture indicates we should be joyful just for the simple fact we're having to grow and persevere. James, the early leader of the Jerusalem church and half-brother of Jesus, writes: *"Consider it pure joy, my brothers and sisters, whenever you face trials of many kinds, because you know that the testing of your faith produces perseverance. Let perseverance finish its work so that you may be mature and complete, not lacking anything"* (James 1:2–4).

James asserts we should be doing *the happy dance* when our faith is tested since becoming mature and complete in our walk with Christ (and the corresponding benefits of confident and blessed living) is only possible through the work of perseverance. I'm not always there, but one thing I notice—when I choose to remember God's promises in the midst of my desert seasons and begin thanking Him for His blessings and solutions to my difficulties, my attitude shifts, my joy returns, and ultimately I can move forward in faith.

Let us be counted among those who in faith believe God's promises and persevere in the mission He's given—no matter what we face. We must remain confident He will come through for us and fulfill His purposes for our lives!

POINTS TO PONDER

1. In what areas of your life are you tempted to give up on an assignment God's given you?

2. How can you encourage yourself to persevere and press through difficult times until you have been released to move on?

3. Is there a promise (call) you've been given for your life? What fulfillment (appointment) are you believing for? How can you

be more deliberate in still accomplishing God's purposes even as you persevere through the "desert" in between?

4. Who are the people God has called to walk with you? Who has God called you to walk with?

PRAYER

"Dear God, I'm so thankful You have a specific plan for my life and I want to fulfill everything You have in mind. Please help me trust and believe You even when the journey gets long and difficult. In my desert journey between Your promises to me and their fulfillment, help me to persevere through such times of transition. May I always continue on this highway You've marked out for me and trust You to remove every obstacle and open every door. In Jesus' name, Amen."

11

TRAVERSING THE MOUNTAIN:
From Despair to Glory

THE SENTRIES POSTED AT THE CITY GATE COULD SEE RUN-
ners in the distance approaching Jerusalem. After their long
journey, the three messengers finally reached the entrance, and
breathless and panting from their hurried run, told the guards
they had an urgent message for the king. After being ushered into
his chambers, the three men delivered devastating news to King
Jehoshaphat: three armies (the Ammonites, Moabites, with some
of the Meunites) were gathering with the intent of attacking and
destroying Judah. Based on the messenger's description of a "vast
army," the odds of defending Judah against this force were very
slim.

What should I do? The king thought. *Our army is terribly
outmatched and we'll be slaughtered. Should I hire soldiers from
another nation? Should we come up with our best military strategy
and just face them anyway? If only I hadn't brought this on us by
going to war with Ahab! The words of the prophet are coming true.*

King Jehoshaphat could vividly remember that disastrous battle. King Ahab of Israel had invited him and the army of Judah
to join the Israelites in fighting the Arameans. Without serious
thought or consulting the Lord, he'd quickly accepted the invitation. *What a mistake!* The Arameans were determined to kill Ahab,
and Jehoshaphat recalled with a shiver how he almost got caught

in the crossfire. Mistaking him for the Israelite King, the Aramean charioteers pursued Jehoshaphat relentlessly. His heart raced in panic as they encroached within shooting range. Before they could draw their bows, however, he cried out, "God, save me!" Such a simple prayer and yet the Lord answered so quickly. Suddenly, even in the fog of war, the Arameans realized they didn't have Ahab in their sights and broke off their pursuit.

The rest of the battle was a blur as Ahab was mortally wounded and the forces of Israel and Judah were routed. Jehoshaphat and his men headed home for Judah in defeat, and then, as they safely re-entered Jerusalem, he was approached by the prophet Jehu who had a message from the Lord.

"Should you help the wicked and love those who hate the Lord? Because of this, the wrath of the Lord is on you," said Jehu.

The prophet's words echoed in his mind as he considered the dire circumstances facing his kingdom. This was his fault. Going to war with Ahab was foolish and had brought great trouble on him and his people. *Would God still be merciful and save them from imminent disaster?* he wondered. Even though the outcome was uncertain, he quickly concluded that asking God for mercy was the only way out. He would "bet the farm" on the Lord's compassion and grace and there was no plan B. They would seek God's salvation and either He would deliver them from their enemies or destruction awaited.

Jehoshaphat quickly gathered his advisers to tell them of his plan. He proposed messengers be sent to every corner of Judah to proclaim a fast and urge men and women from every town and village to gather in Jerusalem to pray and seek the Lord at the temple.

"With all due respect, your majesty," said one official, "gathering everyone together in one place makes us more vulnerable to the enemy's attack. Adding the call to fast makes us even weaker at a time we need to conserve all the strength we have."

"I can understand your concerns," said Jehoshaphat. "However, we really need God's intervention. Our own army and physical strength are completely insufficient to stand against the armies amassing against us. If we humble ourselves, seek the Lord, and repent of our past sins and disobedience, perhaps the Lord will have mercy and save us. It's our only hope."

At the king's command, messengers were sent on the swiftest horses to carry the news to every corner of Judah. Within days, the people obeyed their sovereign and gathered in front of the Lord's temple in Jerusalem—young and old, rich and poor. As Jehoshaphat stood to speak, a hush fell over the crowd as they waited to hear their leader's charge. Instead of addressing them, however, he began praying to the God of Heaven, recalling the Lord's power when He gave them their promised land, drove out their enemies, and promised to protect them from disease, famine, and war if they would cry out to Him in prayer.

With tears streaming down his face, Jehoshaphat recalled the dire circumstances he and his nation were in and asked the Lord to intervene against the invading nations. Finally, lifting his hands in the air and raising his head toward Heaven, the king cried out, *"O our God, will you not judge them? For we have no power to face this vast army that is attacking us. We do not know what to do, but our eyes are on you"* (2 Chronicles 20:12).

The words echoed through the vast throng and briefly hung in the air. Then, everything fell silent. The king continued gazing into the sky with his hands raised while the people stood together as families—husbands and wives, children, toddlers, babies. A slight breeze blew across the strangely quiet crowd. Some stared into the heavens like their king while others bowed their heads and wept. No one said a word. No one knew what would happen next. The earnestness and desperation of the people had Heaven's attention and God was about to answer the king's plea.

Suddenly a voice shattered the silence. Jahaziel, a Levite and worshipper at the temple, had received a message from God for Judah: *"Listen, King Jehoshaphat and all who live in Judah and Jerusalem! This is what the* LORD *says to you: 'Do not be afraid or* discouraged because of this vast army. For the battle is not yours, but God's'" (2 Chronicles 20:15).

Jahaziel then told Jehoshaphat and his army where the enemy would attack and concluded by saying, "You will not have to fight this battle. Take up your positions; stand firm and see the deliverance the LORD will give you, Judah and Jerusalem. Do not be afraid; do not be discouraged. Go out to face them tomorrow, and the LORD will be with you' " (2 Chronicles 20:17).

Immediately Jehoshaphat and the gathered crowd responded with reverence and awe. The king bowed with his face to the ground while all of the people fell down in worship to God. It was a holy moment as some of the Levites stood to loudly praise the Lord for His promised victory over Judah's enemies.

Early the next morning, the army assembled to begin their march to the Desert of Tekoa where the enemy waited. As they set out, King Jehoshaphat stood and encouraged Judah's forces to remain true to the message God had given them the day before. "Listen to me, Judah and people of Jerusalem! Have faith in the LORD your God and you will be upheld; have faith in his prophets and you will be successful" (2 Chronicles 20:20).

He then appointed worshippers to go ahead of the army and praise God "for the splendor of His Holiness," honoring and exalting the Lord as the army went to confront the enemy. Then, something astounding happened. As the sound of singing and praises ascended to Heaven, the enemy's coalition began falling apart to the point where the Ammonites and Moabites joined forces to destroy the men from Mount Seir. They then turned on each other and fought amongst themselves, resulting in the enemy's utter annihilation by their own hand.

As the singers and army crested the hill above the desert valley, they were completely shocked and surprised to see the enemy's dead bodies covering the ground below. It was clear no one had escaped and not a living thing stirred. This complete destruction was nothing short of miraculous and the tension on their faces was replaced by a glow of joy and thanksgiving because of what God had done.

Along with the defeat of their foes, the nation of Judah was blessed with so much plunder (equipment, clothing, and articles of value) that it took three days to collect it all. On the fourth day, all of the people gathered in the place of triumph and praised and thanked the Lord for His incredible goodness and miraculous victory. As a result, that place was called "The Valley of Blessing" (2 Chronicles 20:26b NLT).

Wow! I find this story from 2 Chronicles 20 incredibly inspiring and faith building. I took poetic license in describing how the story transpired, but even that can't come close to illustrating how the place of Judah's potential destruction became a "Valley of Blessing." It's a miraculous story, indeed!

God can do incredible things in our lives when we turn to him for help—snatching us from the jaws of certain defeat and taking us to the heights of incredible joy and victory. Or, if we examine it in terms of our highway analogy, we may be traveling through the deep valley of discouragement and sadness with no hope in sight, only to suddenly find our path begins to climb and climb until we're finally on the top of a mountain that has the most beautiful vista imaginable —a seemingly speedy drive from despair to glory.

This story also teaches us the Lord will even save and deliver us when our own mistakes create our dire circumstances. He doesn't abandon us even when we mess up mightily. (This is certainly good news for me!) In considering Jehoshaphat's rise from disobedience and failure to obedience and success, I see **three key decisions** he made.

First, he **"Gave Up."** As I imagined earlier, when the king first received the news about the attacking armies he had several options. He could:

1. Request help from a surrounding nation and perhaps strike an alliance.

2. Come up with his best battle plan, and even considering his inferior military numbers, do his best to offer significant resistance and perhaps somehow steal a victory. Or,

3. Repent to God for his disobedience, fall on His mercy, and ask for divine intervention in defeating the enemy.

Thankfully Jehoshaphat chose door number three and gave up on his own efforts to win the battle. 2 Chronicles 20 verse 3 says he *"resolved to seek the Lord"* (NIV84). He was going to put all of his energies into pursuing God's intervention. Judah would certainly be defeated unless God took note of the nation's collective humility and responded by showing His strength and power.

Similarly, in our lives we can either:

1. Continue to rely on our own strategies and devices to gain victory in our lives, or

2. Learn when it's time to say "uncle," give up and choose to rely on the Lord instead.

Jonah 2 verse 8 illustrates the importance of rejecting such self-reliance: *"Those who cling to worthless idols forfeit the grace that could be theirs"* (NIV84). An idol is anything we depend upon in times of trouble rather than seeking the Lord and relying upon Him alone; it's anything that takes God's place in our lives and becomes our source.

We can make an idol out of a relationship and put it above our connection with God. Any addiction is also an idol, whether it's entertainment, pornography, the approval of others, or even food. One evening I was stressing about something happening in our church and feeling concern for those involved. As I considered the problem I felt my anxiety level rising. Within minutes I found myself standing in the pantry eating from a large bulk bag of potato chips. Breaking out of my contemplation I looked down at the bag and thought, *What am I doing?* I suddenly realized I was medicating my concern with junk food. At that moment, the junk food had become an idol. No, I wasn't bowing down to it or burning incense. I was, however, substituting prayer and surrender of the problem to God for the taste of the crispy, golden wafers. *(I'm suddenly getting hungry as I write.)*

It's clear from the Jonah 2 passage that we can't depend upon both God and idols. If we continue to steadfastly cling to and depend upon something else, we give up the grace that could otherwise be ours. Grace has been defined as "The God-given desire and ability to accomplish God's will."[1] In other words, when God's grace is active in our lives, we not only have the desire to obey Him and do what's right, but we also have the ability to follow through. Grace is truly amazing and trumps the temporary relief and encouragement idols provide. Proverbs 3:5–6 perfectly sums up the benefits and clarity of such grace-filled dependence: *"Trust in the Lord with all your heart and lean not on your own understanding; in all your ways acknowledge him, and he will make your paths straight"* (NIV84).

Choosing to "give up," therefore, involves letting go of anything—other than God—that we might cling to in our time of need. We choose instead to rely on His grace and strength.

Like Jehoshaphat, such dependence starts by acknowledging our weakness and ignorance. Second Chronicles 20 verse 12 records this important phrase in the king's prayer: *"For we have no power against this great multitude that is coming against us; nor do we know what to do, but our eyes are upon you"* (NKJV).

"We have no power ... nor do we know what to do." While difficult to admit in our culture which honors and promotes self-reliance *(I'm a self-made man! I did it my way!)* this is the starting point in gaining God's strength and wisdom.

Paul the Apostle knew this principle well. As a young man, he was a Pharisee of Pharisees, a rising star in Judaism, and someone of immense skill and talents. In his zeal, he persecuted and killed Christians; however, it took getting knocked to the ground for him to surrender to Christ and begin realizing how insufficient he was on his own. The persecution from religious Jews who disagreed with Paul's message of salvation through Jesus Christ resulted in physical, emotional, and spiritual stress.

After pleading with the Lord three times to take away an undisclosed weakness (something he calls "his thorn in the flesh"), Paul receives an answer from God that would define the rest of his days and should define ours as well.

> *And He said to me, "My grace is sufficient for you, for My strength is made perfect in weakness." Therefore most gladly I will rather boast in my infirmities, that the power of Christ may rest upon me. Therefore I take pleasure in infirmities, in reproaches, in needs, in persecutions, in distresses, for Christ's sake. For when I am weak, then I am strong"* (2 Corinthians 12:9–10, NKJV).

Wow, what a mindset! How differently we'd view our troubles and weaknesses if, like Paul the Apostle, we realized they could become catalysts to receiving even greater strength and grace from God. When we find ourselves way in over our head, the first step is to "Give Up."

The second step is given in the last part of 2 Chronicles 20:12, which says, *". . . but our eyes are on you."* Giving up on our own ability and wisdom is useless unless we make a conscious decision to **"Look Up" and focus exclusively on the Lord**—taking our eyes off of the hopelessness of the circumstance and placing them squarely on our Savior. As in Jehoshaphat's prayer, we accomplish this by recalling three things:

1. How great and powerful God is.

2. The awesome things He's done in our lives in the past. And

3. His promised deliverance when we cry out to Him in prayer.

When I focus on problems and obstacles from a natural perspective, I quickly become overwhelmed and lose heart. I feel small and insignificant compared with the circumstances around me. I begin to make God big, however, when I worship Him and meditate on who He is. His power and strength are magnified and the view of my problem correspondingly diminishes.

I remind myself of Scriptures such as Psalm 103 verse 8 where it states, *"The LORD is compassionate and merciful, slow to get angry and filled with unfailing love"* (NLT), or Jeremiah 32:27, where He declares *"I am the LORD, the God of all the peoples of the world. Is anything too hard for me?"* (NLT). These passages and many others show that God is always able, and willing, to save us in our distress.

After "making God big," it is then important to recall how He's come through in the past. When we began our church planting journey from Medicine Hat to Calgary, I decided to write down the ways God had provided, opened doors for us, and confirmed His word. I disciplined myself to do this because I knew there would be some very tough days when the pressures of the moment might cause us to question our decision. Having a written record of how God came through in the past would strengthen our faith and resolve to believe for breakthrough in the future.

One such example was how, in the nick of time, God brought our good friends Richard and Margaret Klok to Medicine Hat from Taber, Alberta, to take over The Bridge church (as I shared previously in greater detail). This released us to plant the church in Calgary. The Lord also confirmed we were to leave Medicine Hat through the personal story of a worship leader (as I also described earlier), and through a book called *Halftime* by Bob Buford.[2]

This is exactly what Jehoshaphat was doing when he recounted in prayer how God drove out the previous inhabitants of the land now occupied by Judah. In reminding God of His past exploits and expressing confidence He would come through again, he was also reminding and encouraging all the Jews present. Psalm 96:3 says, *"Publish his glorious deeds among the nations. Tell everyone about the amazing things he does"* (NLT). Writing down and declaring His past exploits builds a confidence that when we cry out in prayer, He'll answer and come through again.

Ultimately, this is what Jehoshaphat was banking on when he called all the people together to fast, pray, and repent. His action is supported by 2 Chronicles 7:14 where it states, *"Then if my people who are called by my name will humble themselves and pray and seek my face and turn from their wicked ways, I will hear from heaven and will forgive their sins and restore their land"* (NLT).

When we "Give Up," forsake our idols, and then "Look Up," the Bible is clear the Lord will hear us and bring healing and restoration into our situation. He'll also redeem the difficult circumstance, transforming it into a blessing (as with Jehoshaphat and the Jewish nation). When we're confident in God's calling and leading in our lives, we can be equally confident He'll ultimately take tough circumstances and use them as stepping stones to take us on to greater maturity and fruitfulness.

We "Give Up" and then "Look Up." Finally, we need to **"Step Up."** Following Jehoshaphat's impassioned prayer to God, the prophet responded with specific instructions about how Judah was to march out against its enemy. The promised victory would only be won if the army stepped out in faith and obeyed the prophet's directives. The soldiers going home and putting up their feet in their proverbial Lazy Boys would not accomplish the task. The prophetic word given was only effective when the people obeyed and followed through.

This is the same in our lives. Our faith and confidence in God are only truly shown when we step out and obey Him in tangible ways. As the Apostle James writes in the New Testament, *"As the body without the spirit is dead, so faith without deeds is dead"* (James 2:26 NIV84). God provided a great victory for the nation when Jehoshaphat listened to God's instructions and the Jewish army marched out and fully obeyed.

Likewise, when we determine to "Step Up" and couple our faith with action, the Lord will bring great victory to our lives and turn certain defeat into success and blessing! Choose to fully depend upon God the next time you encounter a difficult circumstance far beyond your ability and resources. Remember to "Give Up," "Look Up," and "Step Up,"—the keys to seeing your "Valley of Baca" become a "Valley of Blessing."

POINTS TO PONDER

1. In what areas of your life are you overwhelmed and need to "Give Up" on your own efforts to solve the problem?

2. How can you intentionally "Look Up" to the Lord for help? What does that involve?

3. How is God asking you to "Step Up" and move forward in faith so He can bring an amazing victory into your life?

PRAYER

"Dear Lord, I thank You my weakest moments can become my greatest when I put my attention on You. During the difficulties of life, help me "Give Up" on my own efforts to save myself but instead "Look Up" to You for guidance and direction. As I "Step Up" in faith, I believe You will move in amazing ways and bring breakthrough and release in my life. In Jesus' name. Amen."

12

FROM 0 TO 60:
God's Restoration

I SAT OUTSIDE THE BANK IN MY TWO-DOOR WHITE PLYMOUTH Colt. It was a bright, sunny morning, but my mood was exactly the opposite. I was stalling and didn't want to go inside to meet with the mortgage consultant. *He's going to laugh me out of the bank*, I thought. *There's no way I'll qualify for financing. I'm going to be so embarrassed and ashamed.* I had recently started a straight commission sales job and my paychecks were spotty and inconsistent; I didn't have the required two-year track record.

Suddenly, a quiet impression invaded my thoughts. *Just go in. It will be okay. You'll see.* I knew it was the Lord, but it did nothing to silence my fears. Tears stung my eyes as I continued to wrestle with my emotions. Again, that quiet, reassuring impression. *Go in, it will be okay.* Even though I couldn't see what was around the next corner in my life journey, I had to focus on obeying the Lord's prompting and trust that as I moved forward, I would arrive at my destination and things would unfold according to His plan.

My financial position was a far cry from where I was only four years earlier in 1994 while living in Lethbridge, Alberta. At that point, I was a successful insurance agent living in a beautiful house in an exclusive subdivision. And then the bottom fell out of my life insurance sales and I had to relinquish my plum position.

As I've shared previously, we then moved east to Taber to help serve in the church there. I started a vending business, sold it, and then established my ill-fated television magazine publishing business, basically using up all the equity from the sale of my house in the process. Thankfully, we had an affordable rental situation with a house big enough for a growing family of six. But then came a phone call from our landlord in August 1998 that threatened to change everything and complicate our housing situation.

"I've got a proposition for you," Frank (not his real name) said on the other end of the line. "We're going to sell the house and I want to give you the first right of purchase."

My immediate mental response was, *There's no way we could buy it no matter what the cost. We have no money!*

Immediately, however, there was another thought I sensed was from the Lord: *It won't hurt to hear him out and you never know what can happen.*

With that encouragement, Val and I agreed to meet with Frank and see what he had in mind. After driving out to his acreage and exchanging a few pleasantries, he pulled out an appraisal for the house. The house was valued at $124,000.

"However, because you guys are such great tenants we'd like to give you a discount and will accept $114,000. What do you think of that?" asked Frank.

I looked over at him and nodded. "That's very generous," I replied. My thoughts, though, were very different. *I appreciate the reduction but it wouldn't matter how much you lowered the price, WE HAVE NO MONEY! There's no way we can buy this house!*

Again, however, I had an impression: *Just keep walking through this process and see what happens.* I knew it was the Lord encouraging me not to give up too easily. I thanked Frank for his time and told him we'd get back to him soon with our answer. During the next few days, I wrestled with how to respond. *When you have no money, what's a reasonable offer to make? Is there even an offer in such a circumstance?*

Finally, after much prayer and discussion with Val, we settled on an offer of $95,000. We assumed Frank would likely counter at $100,000 (if he wasn't already completely offended by the nearly $30,000 reduction in price) and figured that was the best we could do.

I called Frank and made our offer. Surprisingly, with little resistance, he countered with the $100,000 price. *Now what do I do?* I thought. I hinted to Frank some of the difficulty we might have, and without skipping a beat he said, "Just go see my banker. He's helped me with a lot of deals and I'm sure he can make this work for you."

The next day I called the bank and talked to Frank's consultant. "I'm looking forward to meeting you, Ian," he said. "Please bring your income tax records for the last two years so we have the information to get this deal done." I thanked him for his willingness to meet and ended the call. After hanging up I had this sick feeling in the pit of my stomach. Because I just started a new straight commission job in May, the income tax returns from my last two years meant nothing. Plus, I was barely making a living and my income was sporadic.

Now here I was, wrestling with my fears outside of the bank. Finally, I reached for the file containing my not-so-useful financial information, opened the car door, and stepped out into the bright sunshine. *Here goes nothing,* I thought as I slammed the door and turned to head into the bank.

Sitting down with the advisor, I decided to immediately "come clean." Motioning to the file folder I'd placed on the desk I said, "The information in there isn't relevant to our discussion today. I started a new straight commission job in May, so I don't have the two-year financial track record you're looking for. I don't want to waste your time."

I fully expected him to agree with my conclusion and show me the door. Instead, he said, "Well, let's take a look and see what we can do. I'm sure there's a solution." The advisor began tapping away on his computer and inputting data (which was weird because I hadn't even given him any information). Finally, after a couple minutes he said, "Well, based upon your earnings, and the amount of equity in your house, it looks like we'll need about $7,000 from you to make this deal happen." His response prompted two questions in my mind. *What equity?* and, secondly, *Where will I come up with the $7k?*

The advisor explained that because we were long time, exemplary renters with a good track record, he was treating this like a "rent-to-own" situation with the $24,000 difference between the appraised value and our purchase price becoming equity. That amount, when increased by the additional $7,000, would become a 25% down payment and he could approve the mortgage on the spot. I was becoming excited but still needed the answer to my second question.

"So, do you have $7,000?" he asked. I shook my head and said, "I only have about $3,000" (which is what I figured I could get for my tent trailer—the only significant asset I still had).

He thought for a moment and then said, "You have a line of credit with us, right?" I nodded and then he said, "What if we loaned you the remaining $4,000 from there?"

I was blown away! "Sounds good," I said calmly, hiding my excitement. He printed the documents, I signed off, and that was it. I shook his hand, thanked him, and against all the odds, left the bank with a mortgage. I entered my car a different man from the one who exited with fear and trepidation a half hour earlier. "Thank you, God," I yelled. "You are so faithful!" Amazingly, against all odds, God enabled us to get a mortgage and purchase our house.

As incredible as this story is, however, there was more divine intervention to come as God continued to restore what was lost during my publishing business failure. Two-and-a-half years later, we received the call to lead the Medicine Hat church and it was time to find another house. The first home we placed an offer on fell through, but then our realtor discovered a house two blocks from the Regional Hospital. Because of a fire in the basement, it was freshly painted, with new flooring throughout. It was older, but perfectly fit our budget and had enough rooms for our family of six.

Four years went by and then came another God moment. One warm fall evening, Val and I were out for a walk near a coulee on the Northeast side of our city. Walking through a golden field with sun-dappled hills to our north and elegant, gorgeous houses to the south, I was suddenly reminded of our Tudor house in Lethbridge. Although thankful for the home God provided us in the Hat, there were times I longed for the newer dwelling we once owned, with its comfort, double car garage, and fenced yard.

I would sure like to own a house like that again, I thought wistfully as I surveyed the beautiful dwellings lining the coulee. Almost immediately I heard that still small voice in my spirit. *I know,* I sensed the Lord saying. He wasn't rebuking my longing for our former home but was validating those feelings and saying He was going to do something about them. Psalm 37:4 says, *"Delight yourself also in the* LORD, *And He shall give you the desires of your heart"* (NKJV).

I was walking slightly ahead of Val, so I immediately turned and walked back to share my thought with her. "Honey, I think the Lord just told me He understands our desire for a better house. And ... I think He's planning to do something about it," I said. She shared my excitement at the idea of God providing us a newer house, so we both decided to tuck that impression away in our hearts and see what God might do.

Val and I were currently aware that because of the proximity to the hospital, houses in the area we lived were being bought and converted into offices by doctors and other health professionals at selling prices greatly above average. Our home was particularly desirable because it faced a main thoroughfare and was highly visible. We began to wonder if God might somehow use the location to satisfy our desire for a better and bigger house.

Several months later, in the spring of 2005, we began seeing God work to make our dream come true. We were sitting in the stands of the Medicine Hat Fieldhouse watching our son Russell play indoor soccer. With less than four minutes left in the game, I was having a great chat with a realtor in the city whom we'd gotten to know while attending our son's sporting events.

As we sat there, I suddenly sensed another impression from the Lord: *Tell him about how close your house is to the hospital and how it would be ideally suited for a doctor's office.* My initial thought was, *It's a little late now. The game's almost over!*

I obeyed the prompting, however, and leaned over to share my thoughts with him. As the game wound down he replied, "How about I call you in a week about that, Ian?"

"Great," I said, unclear by his expression as to whether this would go any further.

As we stood and began filing out I turned to Val, who had been sitting with a friend two seats to my right, and told her about my impression and then chat.

"Yes, I heard you talking with him about the house," she said. "Funny thing is, just a couple minutes before you started talking I also sensed we should make him aware of our house location and our desire to sell."

"Wow," I said. "God is definitely up to something. Let's see what happens."

True to his word, within a week the realtor called and told us he had someone interested in exploring the purchase of our house as a doctor's office. "Coincidentally," he'd been asked to find such a property just prior to our visit with him.

"God's timing is perfect," I said to Val after hanging up the phone. "He has someone very interested in purchasing our house. This could be the break we're looking for."

Indeed, it was. Within ten days the prospective buyer toured our house twice and he and his wife decided to make the purchase. Without putting a dime into upgrading the house (we had very little money to spare) we made nearly a 50% return in just over four years.

After the sale, we turned our attention to the search for our next house. We toured home after home with no success. There was always some detail that didn't fit with our plans, and inner peace continued to elude us. From experience, Val and I have learned God will guide us in our decision making by the presence, or lack of, peace.

The possession date for the owners of our home was fast approaching and we still hadn't found a new place to live. I tried not to worry about that but instead kept trusting the Lord had a plan. It's amazing how the answer to our prayer can be right under our noses, as it were, and we can't see it because of our own biases and preconceived notions. That was the case with me.

A young woman in our church named Anya had been asking me for a couple of months to check out the house her father was selling. Each time I politely declined because I didn't think the house was suitable for us. Truthfully, I thought it would be too expensive for us. As well, the back faced the Trans-Canada highway and I thought it would be too noisy. Amazingly, I'd never even gone to take a look.

As always, God was gracious to our family. One last time Anya asked us to view the house. "Do it as a favor to me," she said. We therefore decided to help her out and we went as a family to tour the house. One by one the boys piled out of the van and entered the vinyl sided white and grey bi-level house with six bedrooms and attached and detached two-car garages. We were in love! The boys oohed and awed as we entered room after room. As I stood in the basement looking out the big, bright windows and marveling at the size of the house and the amount of garage space, I sensed this was it. I had a peace and excitement confirming we had come home. Val and the boys agreed and we made an offer we could afford—and it was accepted!

Amazing! In seven years, we'd gone from a rental situation in Taber with very little income and almost no savings to a position where we owned a beautiful home and had nearly $150,000 in equity. God can indeed restore that which is lost in the challenging times of our lives.

The biblical story of Job highlights this principle. He was blameless, upright, feared God, shunned evil (Job 1:1) and was one of the richest and most powerful men of Arabia in the middle east[1] around 1700 B.C.[2] There was a season, however, when his life highway traveled through a very lonesome and desolate valley. He lost his health, wealth, and much of his family—despairing even of life.

After these intense trials, however, Job comes to see and know God in a completely different light. After an encounter with His Creator, he exclaims, *"My ears had heard of you but now my eyes have seen you"* (Job 42:5). Following this revelation, the Lord restores Job and gives him twice as much as he had before (Job 42:10) and the latter part of his life became more blessed than the former (vs. 12).

When our journey takes us through such difficult places, it's vital that even in the uncertainty, we position ourselves for breakthrough by obeying and trusting in the Lord's guidance and faithfulness. Despite outward circumstances, where it seems everyone and everything is seemingly against us, we need to believe when we continue obeying the Lord and trusting His Word, He will ultimately lead us into a destiny much bigger than ourselves. He has blessings and good things for His children and will ultimately work all things out for our good (Romans 8:28).

The book of Joel also shows God's heart of restoration even when our loss and pain are the results of our own sin and disobedience:

"So I will restore to you the years that the swarming locust
    has eaten, . . .
You shall eat in plenty and be satisfied,
And praise the name of the LORD your God,
Who has dealt wondrously with you;
And My people shall never be put to shame.

                (Joel 2:25–26 NKJV)

In this passage, the Israelites have experienced a time of great devastation because of their disobedient actions. However, once they turn to the Lord with all their heart (vs.12) He promises to restore what was lost. The same is true for us. At times, we may stray from the path God's marked out for us and go our own way—with the result being leanness and lack. When we repent and return to Him, however, He promises to restore us to a place of plenty so our hearts are glad and we marvel at His goodness.

Not convinced yet? Here's one last passage that shows God's intent:

". . . when you and your children return to the LORD your God and obey him with all your heart and with all your soul according to everything I command you today, then the Lord your God will restore your fortunes and have compassion on you . . ." (Deuteronomy 30:2–3).

Whatever your disappointments and losses, I encourage you to turn your heart back to our compassionate God and believe He can and will restore what was taken.

POINTS TO PONDER

1. Where have you experienced reversals and loss but need to begin believing God for restoration?

2. Is there disobedience or known sin in your life that's preventing the Lord's blessing? If so, how can you make it right with God and others?

3. Are there any steps of faith (toward restoration) that God's asking you to take now—even though you can't see around the next corner of your life journey?

PRAYER

"Dear Lord, thank You for being the God of restoration. Even if the loss in my life is because of my own sin and disobedience I know You can restore as I humble myself, repent, and serve You once more. Please forgive me for the moments when I've walked my own way or have doubted Your goodness. I ask that my eyes would see You again and that I would live in the reality of Your restorative power. I thank You no matter what failures and setbacks I've endured, I will eat plenty, be satisfied, and never be put to shame as I place my trust and confidence in You. In Jesus' mighty name. Amen."

13

FREEDOM TRAIL:

Understanding
the Father's Heart

Tears streamed down my cheeks as I rushed through the hospital lobby with my mother. "Would you like a pop?" she asked, trying to cheer me up. I avoided eye contact and vigorously shook my head as I tried suppressing the sobs wanting to escape. Keeping my head down, I resolutely continued out the front door and through the parking lot to our car. Thoughts swirled in my mind as I considered what had just happened.

I'll never see my dad again! That's the last time we'll be together on this earth and those were the last words I'll ever say to him! How will we make it? What will our life be like now?

Entering our Pontiac Ventura Sedan, I continued trying to hold myself together as my mother started the car and began making her way out of the parkade. Only after she left the lot and turned onto the street did I finally break down and weep. At my mother's suggestion, I had just said my final goodbyes to my father who was dying of liver cancer.

The countdown to this moment had started six months earlier, April 1977, when I overhead a conversation between my parents. My dad was reporting the results of his doctor's appointment that afternoon—a cancer checkup. Four years earlier, surgeons had removed a malignant mole from his left leg and he underwent chemotherapy. During the next three-and-a-half years, he enjoyed relatively good health and experienced no further symptoms. The yearly checkup was a formality—or so he thought.

After a battery of tests, the doctor was close to declaring him cancer free but decided to run one more on his liver. My father broke the news as the afternoon sun streamed through our kitchen window and my mother stood at the sink washing dishes. "My liver was full of nodules," he said referring to the discovery of multiple cancerous polyps. At the time, I didn't fully recognize the gravity of that devastating news, but in six months I would. Like an embedded enemy agent, the cancer had remained undetected and then chose to attack his liver. It was terminal. No cure. Now he was in the last stages of the disease, and, barring a miracle, it was just a short time before he would leave us for Heaven.

I was twelve years old, and except for that late afternoon revelation (which I didn't fully understand at the time), my mom and dad chose to withhold the full scope of the illness from my older brother and me, choosing instead to pray for a miracle and live life to the fullest. My lack of understanding led to much frustration when my father spent most of our August Vancouver holiday resting in bed and only occasionally getting up to go with us for some sightseeing or tourist activity.

Now it was four days before his death. Although I suspected he might die, there's a difference between suspecting and being pulled aside in the visitation room and being told your father isn't going to make it and likely won't be conscious much longer—so this is probably the only opportunity to say goodbye.

How does a 12-year-old say farewell to his father? Wisely, my mother said to tell him "I'll see you again sometime" at the end of my visit. Of course, the "sometime" would be when my life was over and I met my dad again in Heaven. It was good advice and "I'll see you again sometime" became the last words to my father, David Kenneth Byrd.

My parents believed for a miracle. Jesus healed many in the Bible and my mom and dad heard modern-day testimonies of those who received His healing touch and were made whole. They also attended numerous meetings where people laid hands on my dad and prayed for God to heal him of the cancer. But it was not to be. My father's healing awaited him in Heaven.

The day after his death, as I sat around our kitchen table with my mother and a couple of others, I was told something that gave me great hope for my future. "Ian, I want to encourage you with something," said Marion, my mom's best friend. "The Bible says God is a father to the fatherless and a defender of widows. He'll be your dad now, and you don't need to feel alone or abandoned. He'll take care of you." Those words were great comfort and I truly wanted to fully grasp this truth and know the Lord as my father, yet I still had to grapple with the grief and disappointment of losing my earthly dad.

As the months and years went by, it seemed like life was dog-piling one challenging situation after another upon me, making it even harder to relate to God as my Father. As previously described, when I was 20 and Val 19, her parents were suddenly killed in a tragic car accident. And then, when I had reached the age of 31, my mom passed away from the debilitating effects of successive strokes. The deaths of all our parents, coupled with other struggles and failures, served to reinforce my belief that I needed to take care of myself rather than trust in God's care and attention. This further pushed me away from a healthy understanding of the caring heavenly Father Marion had described that night.

In spite of my difficulties, however, the Lord has done a great work in my heart, and now the unconditional acceptance and the unchanging faithfulness of His Fatherhood is especially real to me. I will share a bit of my healing journey to illustrate how you too can embrace such transformation in your own life. This will help you to more fully experience the love of the Father and enable you to become a highway transporting that love to others.

Let's first examine how I came to understand God's unconditional acceptance. This was no small feat, considering my upbringing. Yay God! Although I don't wish to dishonor my late father, I do need to mention he was a perfectionist who had very high expectations about my performance. Nothing was ever quite good enough, and he rarely congratulated me on my achievements. Friends of our family, however, would sometimes mention how my dad had told them I was near the top of my class and having great academic success. These back-door compliments were somewhat gratifying, but I always longed to hear them directly from him. A particular incident in grade one exemplified his mindset and for years drove my quest for perfection.

I was a stellar printer who labored to make sure each stroke of my pencil was just right so each letter and word would be perfect. *(Unfortunately, this gifting has not followed me into adulthood, as my penmanship is now more like that of a doctor than a champion grade one scribe.)* I was slow but I was good—and I knew it! I was therefore not surprised when one of my masterpieces was chosen to be hung in our classroom during the parent/teacher night—only one of three picked for the "wall of fame." I was thrilled at the thought of parents filing through our homeroom and oohing and awing at the amazingness of my handiwork. I imagined how my father would smile and relish that his son's printing was highlighted for excellence. *This is going to be so good,* I thought.

When the big night arrived, I could hardly contain myself as I waited for my parents to return from the school. *Will they see my printing? What will they think? Will my dad be pleased?* Finally, I saw our car enter the driveway and knew they were home. Eagerly I watched through the window as the car and headlights were shut off and my parents exited and headed up the back steps. They'd barely entered the house and were still taking off their coats when I turned to my dad and with great excitement and anticipation said, "Did you see my printing on the wall? What did you think?"

As he continued hanging up his coat he said, "It was good.

However, it did look a bit crooked." And that was it. He turned and walked into the living room as the smile faded from my face and excitement drained from my soul. I was discouraged and dismayed as I considered what I'd learned from the evening.

I had worked so hard on that printing. I had given it everything I had and had done the best I could, but it still wasn't good enough. Even when I do my best it's not good enough. I must try harder, I must work harder, and maybe someday what I do will be good enough—it will be perfect!"

My already perfectionistic tendencies were greatly reinforced that evening. The conclusion that was reached and the lie that was believed became my driving force for years to come. Amazing, isn't it, how one careless response from my father when I was seven could have had such long-lasting impact! I'm confident he didn't mean to hurt me or incite a quest for perfection, but unfortunately, that's what had happened. It highlights how all of us must weigh carefully what we say, especially as parents when we respond to the successes or failures of our children. Will we show unconditional acceptance and affirmation even when our children disappoint us? Can we correct them lovingly without wounding their spirits and crushing their hopes? As the Bible says, *"Death and life are in the power of the tongue, And those who love it will eat its fruit"* (Proverbs 18:21 NKJV).

My drive for perfection finally came to a head in my early thirties. As I attempted to pioneer a new television magazine franchise, (as per previous description), and sell enough advertising to adequately launch it, I reached the limits of my emotional and physical capacity. Up to that point, I was always able to gut out my difficulties, persevere, and ultimately succeed and excel—in high school, college, and in my employment opportunities.

This time, however, I was staring failure in the face and I was the one going to blink and say "uncle." Try as hard as I might, I definitely wasn't going to get this printing straight enough. Worse yet, my imperfection would be highly visible on the wall of my life and I was terrified everyone would see it. I felt like I was on the edge of a cliff staring into a dark abyss of hopelessness, concerned any minute I would completely lose my footing, plunge into that dreadful pit, and be forever deemed an utter loser. This incredible fear of failure, and my need to excel at all costs finally drove me to my knees where I asked the Lord to reveal the root of this mindset. It was here He graciously showed me the impact of my father's statement, along with other moments in my life where words and actions reinforced this perfectionist thinking.

To gain freedom I then did two things:

1. I forgave my dad for his careless comments that dark night in Southern Ontario. Even though he passed away long before, for my sake it was important I release him and thereby release myself from any lingering hurt and bitterness.

2. I asked God to forgive me for using that incident as a basis to believe that nothing short of perfection was acceptable. I then broke agreement with that belief and declared the new truth I would embrace. I said something like, "Lord please forgive me for believing I must always live and perform perfectly to be accepted by You and others. Father, I now reject that lie and choose to believe You unconditionally accept and value me regardless of my performance. I am Your son and I walk in Your full approval and love. Amen."

I wish I can tell you those prayers were the end of the matter, but to be truthful, they were really just the start. Expressing those things to God broke me free from old lies and beliefs, but because of our culture and the world we live in, I will always need to guard and remind myself of this truth of God's unconditional acceptance.

As John Dawson, International President of Youth With A Mission (YWAM), writes, "We live in a performance-oriented society. Acceptance is always conditional—*if* you make the football team, *if* you bring home a good report card, *if* you look pretty, *if* you have money, *if* you win. The kingdom of this world is a kingdom of rejection. The Kingdom of God is a kingdom of unconditional love. God's promises are conditional, we must obey Him to see blessing, but His love is unconditional."[1]

In addition to understanding God's unconditional acceptance, I've come to realize He's an incredibly faithful Father who will never leave nor forsake me. As I stated earlier, I wanted to believe what Marion told me the day after my father died; God was now my father and I didn't need to feel alone or abandoned. However, agreeing with that statement in my mind was very different from truly believing it in my heart and living in that reality.

Because of all the subsequent losses I detailed earlier, as a married man and father of four sons, I still struggled with feeling abandoned and orphaned all the way into my late 30s. In a strange way, I always felt displaced and never truly at home—like I was constantly trying to figure out my role in the world and yet there wasn't really one for me. Strange indeed! I sometimes found it hard to confidently connect with others, or even fully engage with my own sons, believing even they didn't want me or need me. In particular, I found it difficult to see myself as a fully accepted child of God.

Thankfully, the Lord brought someone into my life that was knowledgeable and gifted in helping people find healing from such an orphan mindset. His name is Dennis Wiedrick, and I vividly remember our time of prayer together. He was a guest speaker at our Medicine Hat church, and I was touring him around our city in my late model Dodge Caravan. As we chatted and enjoyed the sights, he started to probe and prod me a bit.

"So Ian, how do you view God?" he started. "Do you see Him as a loving Father or do you struggle to believe that He really accepts you and is pleased with you?"

I had to admit the latter was true. I rarely sensed God's acceptance and love but often felt detached and that I didn't measure up.

"Ian, you're living like an orphan," Dennis continued. "You have full rights and privileges as a child of God, but you don't believe it and aren't walking in them. Instead, you feel abandoned, isolated, and like God doesn't care."

Tears welled up in my eyes as he accurately described my condition. I didn't feel like a favored son who had his father's complete attention and love—but I so desperately wanted to! Sensing he was striking a nerve and the Holy Spirit was beginning to do some healing in my heart, Dennis asked if I was ready to do business with God and deal with the issue. I said "yes" and began to choke up as I thought of the possibility of finally being free. I then parked the van and Dennis took me through a two-step prayer process:

1. I repented to God for believing I was orphaned, abandoned, and not truly one of His sons. I asked His forgiveness for making such judgments based on my past experiences.

2. I then accepted He truly was my father. I said something like, "Lord, I know You made me to have a true Father-son relationship with You and today I embrace that truth in my own life. I am a favored son who's loved unconditionally. I affirm You will always be with me and never abandon me. Because of this truth, I am safe and secure and can love others the same way. Thank You that I can love my sons, and receive their affection and acceptance because I'm Your son. In Jesus' name, amen."

I instantly sensed a shift in my heart after I prayed those prayers. I knew something had happened and I'd never be the same. To put an exclamation point on the occasion, Dennis gave me a big hug and as he held me tightly whispered in my ear, "The Father loves you, Ian. You are his favored son!" The prayers, the embrace, and the words made a permanent change in my heart and I began seeing myself as a son rather than an orphan.

I'm not the only one to deal with this orphan mindset. There are many in our world who've been separated from their fathers because of death, divorce, or abandonment of the family. Others are "orphaned" by their parents' careers or suffer great disappointment and hurt because of numerous broken promises or neglect. These experiences can cause us to distrust our Father God who always keeps His Word, is consistently loving, and desires to show us that unconditional love and forgiveness for all of eternity. Psalm 27:10 states, *"Though my father and mother forsake me, the LORD will receive me."*

John Dawson continues to explain the Father heart of God as he ties two Scriptures together where God shows His absolute faithfulness to us: He says, *"I will never desert you, nor will I ever forsake you... I am with you always, even until the end of the age"*[2] (Hebrews 13:5; Matthew 28:20 NASB).

People will let us down and set a bad example, but God is only interested in our best. Jesus declared, *"I came so they can have real and eternal life, more and better life than they ever dreamed of"* (John 10:10 MSG). If you're not experiencing such a life, don't be condemned or discouraged. It's time for you to understand that God is for you and completely committed to your success: *"Even when we are too weak to have any faith left, He remains faithful to us who are part* of *Himself and He will always carry out His promises to us"* (2 Timothy 2:13 TLB).

If this chapter strikes a chord, I encourage you to use my prayers earlier in this chapter as a template and allow God to heal you and give you confidence about His unconditional acceptance and unwavering faithfulness as your heavenly Father.

POINTS TO PONDER

1. Ask the Lord to reveal the root of any mindsets you have, or lies you're believing, that are holding you back from experiencing His full love and acceptance as your heavenly Father. What are these roots and what impact are they having on your present life?

2. Is there anyone you need to forgive or ask for forgiveness regarding these issues?

PRAYER

"Lord, please forgive me for believing I must always live and perform perfectly to be accepted by You and others. Father, I now reject that lie and choose to believe that You unconditionally accept and value me regardless of my performance. I am Your son/ daughter and I walk in Your full approval and love. I know You made me to have a true Father-son (Father-daughter) relationship with You and today I embrace that truth in my own life. I am a favored son/daughter who's loved unconditionally. I affirm You will always be with me and never abandon me. Because of this truth, I am safe and secure and can love others the same way. Thank You that I can love the people in my life, and receive their affection and acceptance because I'm Your son/daughter. In Jesus' name. Amen."

THE HIGHWAY OF HEROES:

What's in Your Hand?

A LONE FIGURE WALKED ACROSS THE WIND-SWEPT DESERT, followed by a straggling herd of sheep. His steps were strong and steady for an 80-year-old man. In his right hand, he held his staff, a weathered piece of wood used as a walking stick, as he strode through the sand and began his climb up the rocky terrain of Mount Horeb in Arabia.

In another life, he lived as a prince enjoying the finest food, clothing, culture, and education. He was groomed for leadership and had thoughts of grandeur and influence, of making a difference, and saving his people from oppression. But that was forty years ago. His moment had come and gone; the flame of his leadership—extinguished by an impetuous attempt to fulfill his destiny —too little too soon and now it was too late. Forced into exile, nothing was left of that prince. The winds of time had swept him away without a trace, just like his fresh footprints quickly vanished in the desert gale.

It wasn't all bad. In this barren land, he had thrived. He had found a good wife, started a family, and grew content—even satisfied with his role as a shepherd. The hours and days on his own provided time to examine his motives and reconsider his priorities. He came to realize pride and self-assurance marked his earlier life. He thought he knew everything, but now, in the isolation of the desert, he realized he understood nothing. Broken and humbled, he would be grateful to live out his days in seclusion and watch his children, grandchildren, and great-grandchildren grow up.

Clutching his staff tightly, he hiked further up the mountain, carefully picking his way through the rocks as he sought fresh pasture for his herd. And then, *it happened*. In the distance, he saw the orange glow of a brush fire, which was not uncommon in this desert furnace; but this one seemed different. As he approached, he noticed that even amidst the heat and flames the bush was not burning. Something, or in this case, someone, other than the dry branches and leaves was providing fuel for the blaze. Puzzled, he moved closer, trying to determine the mysterious source.

Suddenly, the crackling fire was trumped by a voice from within the bush. *"Moses, Moses!" it said.*

"Here I am," he replied, startled and afraid.

"Do not come any closer ... Take off your sandals, for the place where you are standing is holy ground. . . I am the God of your father, the God of Abraham, the God of Isaac and the God of Jacob" (Exodus 3:4–6).

Terrified to look at God, Moses hid his face.

———

What follows in Exodus 3 and 4 is God's calling of the man who became Israel's great deliverer from Egyptian slavery and bondage, a dialogue where Moses expresses his doubts and fears and God patiently promises His presence and power to fulfill the task. Prior to the Lord winning the debate, Moses wondered aloud what to do if the elders of Israel and members of Pharaoh's court didn't believe he spoke for God.

> Then the LORD said to him, *"What is that in your hand?"*
>   *"A staff," he replied.*
>   The LORD said, *"Throw it on the ground."*

> *Moses threw it on the ground and it became a snake, and*
> *he ran from it. Then the* LORD *said to him, "Reach out your*
> *hand and take it by the tail." So Moses reached out and took*
> *hold of the snake and it turned back into a staff in his hand.*
> *"This," said the* LORD, *"is so that they may believe that the*
> LORD, *the God of their fathers—the God of Abraham, the God*
> *of Isaac and the God of Jacob—has appeared to you"* (Exodus
> 4:2–5).

Following these instructions, Moses later used this miracle to confront Pharaoh and display his God-given authority.

Something else in this story stands out. Notice the Lord answered Moses' insecurity and fear by directing attention to his staff, which was not only a shepherding tool but also a symbol of his walk with God in the wilderness. By asking Moses, "What is that in your hand?" I think the Lord was showing him his forty years of faithful service would now become a foundation for future success. God then had told Moses to throw it down—surrendering that hard work and labor. Moses had obeyed and released his staff and, by extension, his life to the purposes of God. What followed was a miracle; a change so significant the weathered walking stick would later be called the *"Staff of God"* (Exodus 4:20). With his God-given authority, Moses eventually used the staff to split the Red Sea and lead the people of Israel out of Egypt on dry ground.

This is a powerful picture of what God wants to do in each of our lives. Faithfulness and perseverance during our desert times become the launching point for a greater purpose. What may appear mundane and meaningless suddenly has new significance when empowered by the Holy Spirit in a fresh life season.

If we don't persevere in the difficult times, it may leave us unprepared for the next step. When it was David's time to become Israel's king, in his "hand" was leadership of a rag-tag army of men who became seasoned warriors as they fled King Saul in the wilderness. Touched by the power of God, they became the government of the nation. In Joseph's "hand" was exemplary service to Potiphar (in spite of the false accusations of the Egyptian's wife) and his impeccable management of the prison where he was captive. When surrendered to the Lord's purposes, these experiences became the supernatural ability to wisely prepare a nation for a season of great famine and drought. This provided salvation for Joseph's own family—God's chosen people, the Israelites.

When I think back I realize there were times when I could have lost heart, abandoned my desert experiences, and let go of the dreams God had placed inside of me. I was only able to persevere because of confidence in His promises to give me a hope and a future (Jeremiah 29:11). I also asked the Lord to help me have a big picture perspective about the work He was accomplishing in my life. What larger purpose was on the other side of this time of stretching and preparation? What were the skills I was learning which would enhance my ability to bless others and fulfill my calling in Christ? In the meantime, was I being disobedient to Him in any way or harboring any wrong attitudes or sin in my heart?

On the reverse side of a tapestry, there's nothing to see that makes sense or has any visual appeal—no discernable order to the tangled mess of brightly colored threads. Turn the tapestry over, however, and these apparently random threads become key elements in a wonderfully designed masterpiece of brilliant color with carefully crafted shapes and images. I remember wondering how the threads of my ten years of varied business endeavors and life experiences would weave together and produce a discernible picture. Then came the day when Val and I were called to lead a local church—the fulfillment of a longtime dream. Things suddenly were clear as I was finally looking at the other side of the tapestry.

Considering our new calling, the various "threads" of preparation and testing made sense. I could see how my work in sales gave me the relational skills necessary to deal with difficult and demanding people (not that church people are ever that way). My pioneering of the TV Facts magazine (even though it ultimately failed) trained me in perseverance and how to cast vision and persuade others to buy-in—again an important part of church leadership. And finally, those years away from full-time church ministry were humbling and helped me realize my gifting and dreams were from the Lord. I now knew I couldn't make anything happen on my own but had to fully submit to His timing and will—once again, a vital revelation for someone leading a local church.

God wants all of us to similarly understand He's ordering our lives as we submit to Him and His purposes, using every circumstance for our ultimate good (Romans 8:28).

You may be asking, "Ian, how can I be more aware of what the Lord has placed in my hand? I want to be faithful and steady in the purposes of God for my life, but I just don't know what those gifts and abilities are."

I like what Pastor Rick Warren, founder of Saddleback Church in Orange County, California, has to say about this. He teaches God has given each of us unique **SHAPE** so we can benefit and be a blessing to others. These are defined by him as **S**piritual Gifts, **H**eart, **A**bilities, **P**ersonality, and **E**xperiences.

Rick says, "We're all a part of the body of Christ, and each part matters. There are no insignificant people in the family of God. You are shaped to serve God, and He is testing you to see how you are going to use the talents He gave you. Whether you are a musician or an accountant, a teacher or a cook, God gave you those abilities to serve others."

He continues, "Like the parable of the talents in Luke 19, if you don't use what God has given you, He will take it away and give it to someone else who will. But if you use your talents wisely, God will give you more."[1]

I'm confident that, like me, you want to be a wise steward effectively using your gifts and talents for God's purposes. With that in mind, I will briefly unpack **SHAPE** so it can be a tool helping you achieve that goal.[2]

In assessing how God has designed you, the first place to start is:

S – Spiritual Gifts

What has God supernaturally gifted you to do? As Paul the Apostle wrote to the church in Corinth, *"Now about spiritual gifts, brothers, I do not want you to be ignorant"* (1 Corinthians 12:1 NIV84). We need to take that admonition seriously and avoid the tragedy of never using the special abilities the Holy Spirit gives us in serving others and strengthening His people. (Please see Romans 12 and 1 Corinthians 12 for an extensive list of these gifts). This spiritual gift discovery can occur through experimenting. Or, as the guide "S.H.A.P.E. – Assessment to Assist in Serving" explains, "It's easier to discover your gift through ministry than to discover your ministry through your gift." In other words, just start loving and serving other people and see what strengths surface.

I remember when my son Cacey (#3) had an opportunity to speak at a youth event hosted by another church. He was seventeen and hadn't shared in such circumstances before. In spite of nervousness, however, he stepped out in faith and spoke the message God provided. When he finished, Val and I were astounded. He was a natural and sounded like he'd been preaching for years. The experiment worked and he's never looked back!

Discovery can also happen by studying some of the great books about spiritual gifts and/or taking one of the many assessments available. (Please see the end of this chapter for the link to a free online test.) Finally, it might be as simple as asking a close friend or associate what they see in you. Often others observe gifts we can't see for ourselves—and can actually call them out of us with their observation and encouragement. Once we consider spiritual gifts, the next step is:

H – HEART

Psalm 37:4 says, *"Delight yourself in the Lord and he will give you the desires of your heart."* Those desires, or passions, ultimately have much to do with our pursuits and how we engage in God's mission. Some questions to ask are: *What drives me?* In other words, what keeps you up at night and pushes you to action? Then it's good to consider, *Who are the people I most want to help? Is there an age or group with whom I have a particular affinity?* Next, *What are the needs I most want to meet for others and why do I enjoy that so much?* And finally, *What cause am I most passionate about? Is there an issue that gets my heart pounding and makes me want to take action?*

I recall a time at Church of the Rock Calgary when our Sunday morning children's ministry was really struggling because of a lack of volunteers—and passion. The small pool of faithful workers was serving since the church started and were becoming weary. They continued persevering, but overall, the ministry was in maintenance mode. Then a group of four women came to our church with a passion to reach children and a drive to take *Kidzrock* to the next level. The original workers retired in peace and this new core began ramping it up. Passion makes all the difference! Next is:

A – ABILITIES

Each of us has skills discovered or learned during our lifetime such as: administrating, coaching, communicating, designing, implementing, managing, negotiating, organizing, promoting, repairing, researching, strategizing, and writing—to name a very few (see the links following this chapter for assessment and complete list). The key is to be honest about what we can and can't do—neither downplaying our skills nor embellishing them either.

As mentioned earlier, for ten years I worked in non-ministry jobs until I was given a church to lead in 2001. As noted, one of those positions was selling television advertising. At the time, I didn't completely see the relevance to my future ministry; however, now I'm very thankful for that role because it taught me the marketing and promotional skills I use in leading our church. Acquired abilities can make a big difference in our effectiveness!

P – PERSONALITY

Understanding this essential part of ourselves becomes the foundation for more effectively expressing the first three qualities—spiritual gifts, heart, and abilities. As Rick Warren writes, "Like stained glass, our different personalities reflect God's light in many colors and patterns."[3] Two personality aspects to focus on are: *How are you energized and how are you organized?* For example, you may be more *energized* by focusing on a goal rather than relationships—or vice versa. Or, you may be more comfortable doing things for people rather than being with people—or, again, the opposite. When it comes to *organization*, you may be someone who prefers to play it by ear rather than sticking to a plan—or vice versa. Or, you may find routine boring rather than restful (like me)—or, again, the opposite.

So far we have: **S** – Spiritual Gifts; **H** – Heart; **A** – Abilities, and **P** – Personality. To cap it all off we finish with:

E – EXPERIENCE

One of my favorite chapters in the Bible (as I share elsewhere in this book) is 2 Corinthians 1. In verses 3 and 4, Paul writes,

> *"Praise be to the God and Father of our Lord Jesus Christ, the Father of compassion and the God of all comfort, who comforts us in all our troubles, so that we can comfort those in any trouble with the comfort we ourselves have received from God."*

This is my, "nothing is ever wasted with God," passage. Even my mistakes or the difficult and challenging times in my life can be useful in helping others once God has brought His healing and comfort to me. With this in mind, what are the spiritual (times you felt especially close to God), painful (problems, hurts, trials), educational (special training and learning), and ministry experiences (your past service) that have impacted your life? Writing these down, along with carefully considering the other SHAPE components, will be very helpful as you begin purposefully moving forward. And, like Moses, if you yield what's in your hand to God's purposes, no matter how small or insignificant it may appear, you will see God supernaturally use it to make a difference in our world. As you are faithful and obedient in serving where He's placed you, the Lord will lead you further into His plans and reveal how the threads of your current life are actually part of the great tapestry of your divine destiny and calling.

POINTS TO PONDER

1. Like Moses in the desert, what are the monotonous and seemingly meaningless tasks in which the Lord is calling you to persevere?

2. What larger purpose may be on the other side of this time of stretching and preparation? What skills are you learning that could enhance your ability to bless others and fulfill your calling in Christ? If you're not sure, ask a close friend or trusted advisor to help you see the bigger picture.

3. What is the unique SHAPE – Spiritual Gifts, Heart, Abilities, Personality, and Experiences – God has given you to fulfill His purposes? How might you more fully explore each of these areas? (For S.H.A.P.E. – 'Assessment to Assist in Serving' – a free test used by permission, please go to my web page *www.iancbyrd.com*.)

4. Ultimately, we need God's help to see the purpose of the "threads" of our experiences and existence. What can you do to intentionally focus on seeking God from this perspective?

PRAYER

"Dear Lord, I thank You for my desert experiences because I know You are with me and will ultimately use them for my good. I ask You to open my eyes so I can see what skills and abilities You have already placed in my hand. Help me faithfully serve You with these talents so I can be ready for the plans and purposes You have for my life in the days and years ahead. I believe You will turn the threads of my life into a beautiful tapestry for Your glory. In Jesus' name, Amen."

15

TAKING THE HIGH ROAD:
The Freedom of Forgiveness

FOR NEARLY THIRTY YEARS HE PAID A TERRIBLE PRICE FOR leading his people's quest for freedom—life in a tiny cell with a straw mat his bed, a bucket his toilet and a small barred window his only visual escape from the dank and depressing surroundings. Grueling daily work in the limestone quarry below, amidst the swirling dust and bright African sunlight, gave him and the other prisoners perpetual "snow blindness," causing excruciating pain. He was only allowed a visit with his wife every six months and would wait ten long years before seeing his two daughters again.[1]

His name: Nelson Mandela.

His crime: leading the resistance against South Africa's apartheid (literally "apartness") racist polices from 1948 to 1994 which, among other things, unjustly separated non-whites into their own living areas, denied travel without a special pass, forbade mixed marriages,[2] and denied non-whites participation in national government.[3]

Mandela's cause was just, but that didn't make his twenty-seven-year prison sentence any less severe.

Eventually, after years of international economic pressure against the South African government, the regime began to fall and Mandela was finally released from prison in 1990 at age 71. A year later, repeal of the racist Apartheid laws began, and in 1994,

Mandela completed his transition from pit to palace with his election as the country's first black president.[4]

All citizens of South Africa (the birthplace of my father and grandfather) were now guaranteed equal protection of the law, full political rights, freedom of expression and assembly, and the right to "choose a place of residence anywhere in the national territory."[5]

Considering the heavy physical and emotional price Mandela paid at the hand of his Apartheid oppressors, it's amazing he not only lacked bitterness toward them but actually championed forgiveness and reconciliation between the races. In the 2009 movie *Invictus*, which tells the story of how Mandela used South Africa's hosting of the 1995 Rugby World Cup as a means to unite the country, Francois Pienaar, captain of the nation's Springbok team, muses about Mandela the night before his team plays in the tournament final. In the scene, Pienaar's girlfriend Nerine walks up and puts her arm around him as he views a beautiful African sunset through the hotel window.

"Thinking about tomorrow?" she asks quietly.

"No. Tomorrow's taken care of, one way or another," says Pienaar, with a heavy Afrikaner accent. "I was thinking about how you spend thirty years in a tiny cell and come out ready to forgive the people who put you there."[6]

Living in bitterness and unforgiveness toward his captors and the racist system that put him in prison was never an option for Mandela. "As I walked out the door toward the gate that would lead to my freedom, I knew if I didn't leave my bitterness and hatred behind, I'd still be in prison," he said later.[7]

Even prior to his release, Mandela's quiet dignity was so impressive the white guards addressed him as "Mr. Mandela"—an unheard-of honor for a prisoner. In turn, he was courteous toward them and addressed each by rank and name.[8] Mandela understood attitudes of bitterness and unforgiveness would hurt his country: "Resentment is like drinking poison and then hoping it will kill your enemies," he noted.[9]

Ultimately, there were only two highways, two national attitudes, that would lead the nation to its destiny. "If there are dreams about a beautiful South Africa, there are also roads that lead to their goal. Two of these roads could be named Goodness and Forgiveness," said Mandela.[10] Likewise, if we are to fulfill our dreams and God's purposes for our lives, then our life-highway must also be marked with those same two qualities.

In the Bible, Jesus shares a powerful account to illustrate how releasing such forgiveness to others is not optional but actually the key to freeing us from emotional prisons. In Matthew 18:22 (NLT), Peter has just asked Jesus how often he should forgive someone for a wrong done against him. "Should I forgive him seven times?" Peter offers, thinking that to be a very generous and gracious effort.

"No, not seven times," Jesus replied, "but seventy times seven! In other words, Jesus implies we should continue to forgive others no matter how many times they may offend us. Four-hundred-and-ninety times is a lot—especially if it's for the same offense!

Jesus then paints the picture of a king who decided one day to bring his business accounts up-to-date and confront the people delinquent in repaying their loans. In the process, a man was brought before him who owed millions of dollars. Unable to cover the vast sum, the king ordered: *that he be sold—along with his wife, his children, and everything he owned—to pay the debt."*

"But the man fell down before his master and begged him, 'Please, be patient with me, and I will pay it all.' Then his master was filled with pity for him, and he released him and forgave his debt" (Matthew 18:25–27 NLT).

So far this is a feel-good story, isn't it? The kindhearted and gracious king has extended incredible mercy to the impoverished man. Sadly, things take a drastic turn for the worse. Immediately after leaving the king's presence, the forgiven man finds someone who owes him thousands of dollars and aggressively pursues a quick settlement:

He grabbed him by the throat and demanded instant payment.

173

"His fellow servant fell down before him and begged for a little more time. 'Be patient with me, and I will pay it,' he pleaded. But his creditor wouldn't wait. He had the man arrested and put in prison until the debt could be paid in full" (Matthew 18:28b-30).

How unbelievable! A man forgiven of millions of dollars is now quibbling with another over a few thousand. Could he not remember the incredible mercy given him and shouldn't he feel an obligation to extend the same grace to his fellow man? Obviously not! Word of this injustice gets back to the palace as witnesses complain to the king.

The Bible goes on to explain the terrible results of such a hardhearted and cold response:

Then the king called in the man he had forgiven and said, 'You evil servant! I forgave you that tremendous debt because you pleaded with me. Shouldn't you have mercy on your fellow servant, just as I had mercy on you?' Then the angry king sent the man to prison to be tortured until he had paid his entire debt (Matthew 18:32–34).

Jesus then gives us *the kicker* to this story. In case we remain in a smug place of judgment, He immediately highlights the implications for each of us if we similarly live in unforgiveness.

"That's what my heavenly Father will do to you if you refuse to forgive your brothers (and sisters) from your heart" (Matthew 18:35).

That last statement puts the fear of God into me. Jesus says our unforgiveness toward others will result in our lives being trapped in a debtors' prison of torment and torture. There's no doubt unforgiveness is a serious heart issue—an obstacle to God building His highways in our hearts and a cancer which festers and multiplies our griefs and sorrows. Any offense committed against us by another human being is relatively minor compared with the incredible forgiveness God has extended to us because of Jesus' sacrificial death on the cross.

Matthew reiterates the importance of forgiveness when he

writes, *"For if you forgive men when they sin against you, your heavenly Father will also forgive you. But if you do not forgive men their sins, your Father will not forgive your sins"* (6:14–15 NIV84).

This is alarming! Extending forgiveness to others is *not* an option. It's mandatory. By harboring unforgiveness, we may think we're somehow punishing the one who has committed the offense against us. In reality, the opposite is true; we're hurting ourselves and keeping our souls in torment and prison. We're preventing the forgiveness and grace of God from extending fully into our lives and from entering the lives of those who have hurt us.

In his book *Healing for Damaged Emotions*, Dr. David Seamands stresses, "The two primary causes of emotional stress are the failure to receive forgiveness and the failure to forgive."[11] We must not only be willing to ask others to forgive us when we wrong them, but, equally important, we must be willing to release forgiveness to others, whether or not they admit their wrongdoing.

If you are resistant to releasing forgiveness because you don't yet feel it in your heart, the key is deciding to forgive first, knowing the feelings will follow later. Forgiveness from the heart is a deepseated action born out of obedience and the exercising of one's will. As Corrie ten Boom, Nazi concentration camp survivor, said, "Forgiveness is an act of the will, and the will can function regardless of the temperature of the heart."[12]

When we release forgiveness to others we must also understand we're not giving approval to their wrong actions nor minimizing the hurt and pain they've caused. Rather, we're removing the opportunity for that event to continue causing us torment and suffering. We are letting go of the pain and the victim mentality, choosing instead to be a survivor.

There are some people who never consider releasing forgiveness to bring healing. They prefer, instead, to *suck it up* and continue walking through life wounded and hurting. I would rather deal with something once and for all, than have it continually raise its ugly face because I ignored it. In doing so, I've learned it's imperative to be honest about instances where someone has hurt me, and then bold enough to talk with that person to resolve the issue. I say "learned" because I haven't always done the right thing and it has cost me.

I recall a time when a friend and I were having dinner at a restaurant with a few others. As we joked and told stories, my friend shared something personal about me that was unknown to the others. The incident was funny and everyone laughed (I can't even remember it now), but I felt hurt and betrayed that my friend would expose me like that just to get a laugh.

For the next day or so I debated whether I should say anything to him. He was such a good friend and I didn't want to unduly hurt him if it was just me being petty and insecure. Ultimately, I chose not to mention it and figured that was it. But, it wasn't. The incident had hurt me and I wasn't being honest about it with either myself or my friend. About six months later, what I buried alive came back to life. My friend was staying at our house and we began a serious discussion about something (again, I can't remember the details) and I inadvertently blurted out something like:

"Well, I want to be able to trust you and feel safe in our relationship but unfortunately I don't. Last fall when we were having dinner at that restaurant you shared personal information with the others—things I'd told you in confidence. That hurt and makes me feel unsafe to share more." My voice quavered slightly and my friend could tell my hurt feelings were real. To his credit, he felt bad and immediately asked forgiveness for the mistake, assuring me it wouldn't happen again. In the spur of the moment he hadn't been thinking about the possible effect of his comments and definitely had no intention of hurting me. I received his apology and we moved on.

The next morning, however, after a good night's sleep and further reflection, he had a challenge for me. "Ian," he began. "Yesterday you told me you didn't feel safe in our relationship because of those things I shared with the others." I nodded, and then he continued. "Well, now I don't feel safe with you." I looked at him somewhat puzzled and then he said, "You waited six months to confront me about this. And now I'm wondering if that's a pattern that will continue? Will you be honest with me in the future or will you harbor unforgiveness at times?"

His comments brought immediate conviction and I realized he was right. Relational safety had to work both ways. As much as he needed to be careful with his comments, I needed to be honest about any hurt or offense I might be feeling. I asked him to forgive me and he graciously accepted.

Overall, I was impressed with his loving candor and so thankful for his friendship. Since that incident, I choose not to let unforgiveness remain. When someone says or does something hurtful, I usually take time to prayerfully consider if I'm being overly sensitive and should just let the matter go, as in Proverbs 19:11: ". . . it is to one's glory to overlook an offense," or if I need to address it. If I sense my hurt feelings are legitimate, however, then I'll arrange a time to talk with the other person and deal with the issue.

The bottom line is we all need to be honest and bold enough to deal with our offenses rather than let unforgiveness fester in our hearts, such as Paul writes in his letter to the Ephesians, *". . . speaking the truth in love, we will grow to become in every respect the mature body of him who is the head, that is, Christ"* (Ephesians 4:15). Ultimately, when we speak the truth in love and give and receive forgiveness, we mature and become more like Jesus.

As an aside, when we ask for forgiveness, I believe it's important we're specific with our request. It's not appropriate to say, "I apologize if I hurt you." That statement doesn't take responsibility; it simply placates another's hurt feelings in an attempt to gloss over the situation. Instead, as my wife and I always taught our children to do, be specific in the apology. Take, for example, the request for forgiveness by my then two-year-old son, Cacey: "I'm sorry, will you please forgive me for opening that present in your closet and then destroying the clock you were getting for Christmas by ripping out its guts so it can never be used again?" Wow, where did that come from? Maybe I still have an issue to deal with!

Still unconvinced as to the importance of forgiveness? Let me quote a study highlighting the many benefits of such a lifestyle. In the InterVarsity Press publication, "Lifeline," the benefits of forgiving were highlighted as follows:

> According to the latest medical and psychological research, forgiving is good for our souls and our bodies. People who forgive: benefit from better immune functioning and lower blood pressure; have better mental health than people who do not forgive; feel better physically; have lower amounts of anger and fewer symptoms of anxiety and depression; maintain more satisfying and long-lasting relationships.[13]

As previously mentioned, God wants to build His highways in our hearts and lives so His love can flow through us to a hurting world—another benefit of forgiving. The mountains of pride and self-sufficiency must be leveled. The low places of depression, insecurity, and fear must be raised up as we forsake our wrong behaviors and forgive others—choosing to become better even when circumstances would try to make us bitter. Nelson Mandela refused to be drawn into negative mindsets and we must do the same. Like him, we can bring much hope and freedom to others if we choose forgiveness and reconciliation as a lifelong practice. As the great civil rights leader Martin Luther King Jr. so aptly said, "Forgiveness is not an occasional act, it is a constant attitude."[14]

We must, therefore, learn the practice of forgiveness. It's interesting to note the king in the parable used in the previous illustration could only forgive the huge debt owed him once he took the time to check his accounts. It was only then he realized a massive theft had occurred—that someone had greatly wronged him. Once he realized the gravity of the situation he had two choices:

1. Demand full payment—which would be impossible for the debtor; or

2. Grant forgiveness and pardon the debt—the action he chose. Because he fully realized his incredible loss, he could then release equally incredible grace and forgiveness.

The same is true for us. To release true forgiveness, we must examine the situation, asking ourselves: "What did I lose? What did this person take from me?" Only after fully grasping this truth can we truly forgive and release them from their actions. This is directly opposed to the conventional wisdom of the world that tells us to forget about the past. Though it's true we are to forget those things which are behind and press on to what lies ahead (Philippians 3:13), that's only possible if we've definitely put those things behind us—if we've truly released forgiveness. If we haven't faced the pain or loss from a past situation and don't fully recognize our need to forgive or be comforted by God, then forgetting about it is just denial and we won't truly be free. Let me give you a personal example to illustrate this point.

My brother Peter is disabled. He was blue at birth due to my mother's extremely long labor; it was likely oxygen deprivation created the brain damage that now impairs his physical and mental functions. Both he and I were born in a small hospital in the town of Sussex, New Brunswick. Had we lived in a larger community with better health facilities, it's likely my mother would have had a cesarean section, which might have averted my brother's difficult birth.

At any rate, even though Peter is two years older than me, I quickly caught up to and then passed him in my development as we grew up. I walked and spoke at an earlier age. I began two grades behind him in school, but eventually, we were in the same class and then, ultimately, I was at least a couple of grades ahead of him.

Throughout our childhood, however, we had a normal relationship just like any other siblings. We played with Lego and our toy trucks and cars, horsed around at night until my mom broke a miniature hockey stick on the bannister (true story), used our Fisher Price figures to pretend we were married with kids and sang songs while my mother played the piano (the cassette reads "The Byrd Brothers Sing Peace Like a River and Other Songs"—still have it).

However, everything changed when I was twelve years old. My dad died, and life became more serious for me. In many respects, I put away my childish things (1 Corinthians 13:11). I no longer played with toys and I began thinking more like a young man. My brother didn't follow me in this, however—he couldn't. He was developmentally stuck and so the distance between us gradually grew. Little brother became big brother and then confidante to my mother in the absence of my father. You get the point. Peter and I would sometimes reminisce about the past, but there was nothing new between us—no common interests, few common relationships, and, overall, little to talk about.

On rare occasions, I would find my young companion again—and just for a moment, we would reconnect as in the old days—like when my first son Addison was born. When Peter first witnessed me holding that little dark-haired baby he exclaimed, "It's just like when we played as kids. Remember Ian? We were married with children!" Tears welled up in my eyes as I saw the excitement in his, and I relived those many times we role-played this exact scenario. I went on to have three more sons, but barring a miracle, it's likely my brother will never be married, nor have kids of his own.

Why do I share this? Because there was a time in my late 20s when the grief of losing my brother (in a relational and emotional sense) hit home. I was stuffing this loss for a long time, but finally one night as I lay in my bed, I could contain it no longer. Sobs wracked my body and I writhed in agony as this deep pain within my soul emerged—my wife praying and trying to comfort me. The Holy Spirit had been drawing me to this point and was now orchestrating my healing.

I expressed my disappointment to God and released my anger at the seeming unfairness of it all. And in a sense, I forgave Him that night. Yes, I realize God did nothing wrong and my brother's disability is not His fault, but nevertheless, I relinquished any perceived right to be angry with Him. As my heart was lanced and the toxins removed, I sensed an emotional release. I began thanking Him for all the ways I was so incredibly blessed—I had a beautiful wife, two sons, and relationships with many others which were deep and satisfying.

I also had a brother, and if I chose, could still relate to him and work to find common ground. Rather than living in self-pity, perpetual grief, and pining for the past, I determined to embrace who he was and the relationship we could still have. Like the king in the parable I shared earlier, I took stock of all that had been taken from me, grieved the loss, but then decided to release the debt and be free. That's the power of forgiveness!

I encourage you to begin listening for what God might tell you in the next days and weeks. As you seek Him and listen to His voice about forgiveness and the preparation of your heart, He will begin showing you the blueprint for further growth and development. Listen and obey what He tells you and I guarantee the rate of His highway construction in your heart will increase. I encourage you to enlist the help of leaders and other mature followers of Christ who can assist and hold you accountable through this process.

My journey toward increased spiritual freedom has always happened with the help of others—whether in a session of prayer or through ongoing relationship and encouragement. If you take the issue of forgiveness seriously and make it a lifelong practice, like Nelson Mandela, you will walk in true freedom and be released from an emotional prison and an island of isolation.

Consider pausing before moving on to the next chapter, and prayerfully reflecting on these questions to determine if God is calling you to take action.

POINTS TO PONDER

1. Whom do you need to forgive and why? What did they take from you?

2. From whom do you need to ask for forgiveness, whether or not they have done the same?

3. From whom do you need to accept forgiveness so you can have peace?

4. Have you continued to beat yourself up over past failures but now need to accept and receive the forgiveness of God and others?

PRAYER

"Dear Lord, I thank You Jesus died on the cross and shed His blood to pay the debt for all my sins. Because I've been forgiven of so much, I can and must forgive others when they wrong me. Please reveal to me, through the power of Your Holy Spirit, if I am holding back forgiveness from someone in my life now, or from a person in my past. Help me determine what I have lost, and walk with me through the grief of facing that. Today I choose to forgive all those who have hurt me in any way. By doing so, I realize I'm not approving or minimizing their wrong behavior but rather, releasing them and myself from a debtor's prison of torment. I pray You would grant them repentance as well and draw them to Yourself. I thank You that as I exercise my will to release forgiveness, the feelings will eventually follow. As I repent of my past mistakes, I also choose to receive Your forgiveness and that of others. I will no longer dwell on the past but choose to walk boldly forward with confidence and freedom. In Jesus' name. Amen."

16

TRAVELLING IN A CONVOY:
The Power of Accountability

I SLIPPED OUT OF BED AND QUIETLY TIP-TOED INTO THE BATH-
room to begin getting ready for the day. For some reason (that I
can't figure out to this day) I decided to leave the light off and rely
solely on the dim early morning haze filtering through the bathroom window. After deciding that showering would wait until I
returned home, I dressed, put on a cap to cover my messy hair,
quickly brushed my teeth, and then headed out of the house for
our church's weekly morning prayer meeting.

Arriving at the church building, I discovered only five of us
were there, including two of my key leaders and a special guest
invited by Garry, one of our regulars. Dave was moving to the city
and was therefore checking us out as a possible church home. A
men's prayer meeting would be a perfect way for him to get to
know the pastor and some of the key leaders.

"It's great to have you with us, Dave. Welcome to Medicine
Hat!" I said, smiling broadly and shaking his hand. The five of us
then sat in a circle around a space heater in the prayer room (the
church building was old and quite cold in late winter). Following
an hour of prayer for our church, city, and each other, it was time
for breakfast at one of the local restaurants—a great opportunity
to catch up on the latest news and strengthen our relationships.

After following everyone out of the church building and locking up, I headed across the road to my red VW Jetta. I was still excited about Dave's attendance and looking forward to getting to know him better at breakfast. I slid into the driver's seat, put the keys in the ignition, and then glanced in the rearview mirror as I prepared to back up. The image staring back at me, however, was mortifying. All around my lips was a wide, chalky white swath—toothpaste! I looked like Bozo the Clown and my embarrassment only deepened when I realized not only had I looked that way throughout the entire meeting, but Dave's first impression of me was this bizarre looking person staring back at me in the mirror. I couldn't believe it. *Well, when I'm getting ready I'll never leave the bathroom light off again! This is humiliating,* I thought. *Dave must think I'm an idiot!* I immediately wiped the residue off with a tissue, but the damage had been done.

After arriving at the restaurant and finding our table, I immediately pulled my two leaders aside. "Why didn't you guys tell me I had white toothpaste all around my mouth?" I asked in frustration. "It was especially embarrassing since this was my first time connecting with Dave!"

"I didn't even notice," said Keith. I stared at him in amazement and then turned my focus to Pete. "Well," he said, "I just thought you must be having a bad day!" *Well, if we'd caught this quickly, I would have avoided embarrassing myself and this didn't have to be a bad day,* I thought.

"Next time something like this happens, please tell me right away," I begged with a laugh.

Now, I realize this is a weird event and I just retold it to all of you and amplified how stupid I can be at times. There is, however, a moral to this story. When God asked Cain the whereabouts of his brother Abel (Genesis 4:9), Cain replied, *"I don't know ... Am I my brother's keeper?"* The answer to that question for us Christ followers is "Yes ... we are!" The Bible is clear in Ephesians 4:15 we are to be *"speaking the truth in love"* so each of us matures and becomes more like Jesus.

This means we each have a responsibility to be honest with our spiritual brothers and sisters when we see blind spots or "toothpaste," as it were. There are times on the highway of life when it may be uncomfortable to lovingly confront someone when they have strayed from the road, but it's the godly thing to do, and it may prevent them from hitting unnecessary hazards. We are our brother's (and sister's) keeper and accountable for how we treat them. Not only must we be attentive to their condition and open to God showing us their needs, we must be bold enough to challenge them when required.

I vividly recall a significant moment when a couple of my Christian brothers called me on some "toothpaste" they noticed in my life. It was the early '90s and I was the father of two little boys aged 4 and 2 (Addison and Russell were the only ones on the scene at that point). In addition to being husband to Val and father of these two very active kids, I was an insurance agent with a growing book of business. In the summer of 1993, I was given my own office in downtown Lethbridge, and trying to establish and build my clientele became a primary focus with a huge time commitment.

Although I was a caring husband and father, I became more distracted and aloof from my family as the pressures of my business mounted. I became less and less *in the moment* and more emotionally unavailable to my wife and sons. I was pre-occupied and not giving them the time they needed. I was unaware of my state until Val finally had enough and drove over to my friend Mike's place to "blow the whistle" on me. Upon arriving home from work that day, I noticed no one was in the house but didn't think anything of it until the phone rang.

It was Mike on the line and with a concerned voice, he said, "Ian, your wife is at our place crying. She doesn't feel cared for by you. She came over here to seek our help." Immediately I could sense defensiveness rising within me as thoughts swirled in my head. *How dare she go over my head and complain to Mike! How embarrassing! She's overreacting. Things are fine at home. Yes, I'm quite busy at times, but it's not as bad as she's saying. I'm not abusive or anything. This is overblown!*

My inner thoughts became my outer response to Mike. He refused to accept my excuses, however, and with a patient tone said, "Ian, you need to do something about this. Why don't Alan (another friend) and I meet with you Friday night to further discuss this and figure out an action plan." Realizing I was getting nowhere and couldn't convince him otherwise, I reluctantly agreed to the Friday meeting and hung up. Inside, however, I was angry and frustrated at this turn of events. I felt so exposed and betrayed by my wife and couldn't fully comprehend where I was going so wrong.

When Val returned home with the boys I immediately asked her why she would do such a thing to me. "Ian," she replied, "I've been telling you for a while that I don't feel cared for and that you're neglecting the boys and pre-occupied with other things, but you haven't been listening. Rather than continue in frustration and disappointment, I decided to go to one of your best friends for help. This is important and I felt this was the only way you would take it seriously and make some changes."

She was right. I did have the tendency to stubbornly continue down the wrong path until I had the proverbial gun to my head. (Unfortunately, I still have that tendency at times.) I needed outside accountability to help me make the lifestyle changes needed to create a healthy environment for my wife and kids.

A couple of days later, I was still struggling with the whole situation as I stood at the sink washing some dishes. *I can't believe this happened, I thought. I feel so humiliated and embarrassed, and I don't understand Val's feelings. I still think she's overreacting. I wish I didn't have to participate in this process!*

Then, as at other important times in my life, I heard this still, small voice whisper truth into my spirit. This time the Holy Spirit said, "Either fall on the rock or the rock will fall on you!" Instinctively I knew what this meant. In the Gospel of Matthew, Jesus was talking about the establishing of the Kingdom of God and referring to the chief cornerstone, His life, upon which this Kingdom would be built. He then goes on to challenge those who oppose Him (the chief priests and Pharisees) to repent. One way or another they will eventually accept His Lordship—either willingly or by force. As Jesus says, *"Anyone who falls on this stone will be broken to pieces; anyone on whom it falls will be crushed"* (Matthew 21:44).

The religious leaders refused to accept Jesus' challenge, however, and instead looked for a way to arrest Him. Likewise, as I stood there by the sink with my dishpan hands, the Holy Spirit was giving me a choice. I could either willingly submit to the loving challenge and correction of my friends, or God would find another way to make me submit and change my ways. To me the solution was clear—I would fall on the rock, or stone, before it had to fall on me!

Decision made, on Friday night I drove to our church building and met with Mike and Alan in a small room. They'd prepared a lifestyle plan to help me function in a more balanced and healthy way, with more time to interact with my wife and children. After I agreed to their proposal and expressed my willingness to be held accountable, we prayed together, asking the Lord to help me make the needed adjustments. I went home and took my initial accountability steps by asking Val's forgiveness for my past behavior and informing her of the agreed upon plan.

The change in my life certainly wasn't instantaneous, but I did see gradual improvement over time as I endeavored to follow the plan laid out for me. In the end, I was thankful for the intervention of my friends and their willingness to hold me accountable for how I stewarded my family.

The Word of God highlights the benefits of such accountability as we walk together through life supported by and in relationship with each other. It's clear the Lord wants us to live accountable to Him and also to each other; as Romans so aptly puts it, *"... none of us lives to himself, and no one dies to himself"* (Romans 14:7).

A Scripture in Ecclesiastes highlights this truth:

Two are better than one, because they have a good return for their work: If one falls down, his friend can help him up. But pity the man who falls and has no one to help him up! Also, if two lie down together, they will keep warm. But how can one keep warm alone? Though one may be overpowered, two can defend themselves. A cord of three strands is not quickly broken (Ecclesiastes 4:9–12 NIV84).

I often quote these verses when conducting weddings because I believe the third strand in any relationship is the couple's intimate bond with the Lord Jesus Christ. He provides the additional unbreakable cord that ensures the marriage *"is not quickly broken."*

Even aside from the marriage covenant, it's important we have friends in our lives who can help us grow in our relationship with God and provide additional strength and resolve in resisting temptation and remaining on the right highway. Such accountability partners ultimately make us better and more effective in our walk with the Lord. Proverbs 27:17 (NLT) says, *"As iron sharpens iron, so a friend sharpens a friend."* There's an element of spiritual sharpness and growth that can only truly be obtained by relating closely with other believers.

We all fall at times in our resolve to serve the Lord and it's at those moments we need the strength of others, along with our own, to get back up, shake off the dust, and continue down the highway the Lord has mapped out for us (Hebrews 12:1). Proverbs 5 admonishes us to avoid adultery and the breaking of our marriage covenant with our spouse. As specific as this passage is, the principles outlined could also apply more broadly and help us avoid life's failures in general.

Verses 12 to 14 express the regrets of the individual who has strayed down the adulterous path only to realize the destructive fruit of those actions.

They say: *"'Oh how I hated discipline! How my heart despised correction! I didn't listen to what my teachers said to me, nor did I keep my ear open to my instructors. I almost reached total ruin in the assembly and in the congregation'"* (GWT). The inference here is those who fail morally do so because they despise discipline, correction, and don't listen to the instruction and admonishment of those close to them. In other words, they fall because they fail to walk in accountability relationships with others.

Accountability is defined as "an obligation or willingness to accept responsibility or to account for one's actions."[1] Yet, the reality is we're only as accountable as we truly choose to be. We can say we're in an accountable relationship with others, but it's a sham if it isn't resulting in regular contact, and happening with complete honesty and vulnerability.

I have two men I hold myself accountable to regarding life issues. If I'm tempted to compromise my standards, I can call them for support and prayer. They have permission to ask me the hard questions about my walk with God, my relationship with my wife and children, and my moral purity. This is a safeguard for my church family and for me.

Starting an accountability relationship may seem like a daunting task, but here are some simple steps and encouragement from the web resource *All About God*,[2] to help you get started.

As with everything else in our Christian walk, it's good to start with prayer. God knows who's best suited to be your accountability partner and will tell you if you ask. It's important to pray for what I call a "divine connection"—a relationship marked with the ease and grace of the Father's touch. As you pray, consider the possibilities within your different spheres of influence. Who in your church, at work, or among your close friends is the Lord highlighting? Look for a man or woman you respect and someone, if possible, who's going through similar circumstances as you—or has experienced them in their past. Accountability can be done in groups of people (so you may be selecting several partners), but when it's in one-on-one situations it's best to select someone of the same gender to avoid any compromising circumstances.

Once you're clear on the Lord's leading, the next step is to explore the connection further. Invite the person to lunch, talk on the phone, or meet each other's family. If it's an existing accountability group you're wanting to join, attend a meeting to see how it goes and to get to know the others. The key things to consider are: do you get along and do you enjoy being together?

Once you're confident this is the right person or group, ask if they will be your accountability friend(s). Be patient with the process. Developing this type of friendship takes time and intentionality. Deliberately participate in activities together and pray regularly for and with one another.

I've found that as the friendship is built, the elements of accountability will just naturally develop. For example, if your friend expresses he's really struggling with spending enough time with his family, then the next time you meet, ask him about that issue. This will start the basic accountability relationship and you can then move on to other matters—holding each other accountable for Bible reading and prayer, physical exercise, matters of integrity, or anything else that surfaces. Obviously, if your relationship is to develop with complete honesty, absolute confidentiality is imperative.

Having a consistent time to talk on the phone or meet together is also vital. Nothing kills an accountability relationship like infrequent connection. Momentum is lost and confidence erodes. A regular day and time is best, but if that's not feasible due to changing schedules, at the end of each meeting always schedule the next one. I've discovered that when I neglect to do this time just gets away, and before I know it, weeks have passed. Such is the nature of living in a busy society.

You may want to read a mutually beneficial book and then discuss portions when you meet. Or, you could do a Bible study on a pertinent topic, or even just bring your journal and share what God's been speaking to you in your quiet times. All of these activities will lead to further discussion and naturally create accountability questions as the relationship develops.

Along with this outside accountability, it's a given we work to maintain excellent communication between us and our spouse (providing we're married, of course). I've found in my relationship with Val that it's vital we maintain true honesty with each other without hiddenness or deception. As the Bible says, it's "the little foxes that spoil the vines" (Song of Solomon 2:15 NKJV). Likewise, compromising on the small issues of integrity will eventually destroy the trust and confidence in a marriage relationship.

When I look back at my life, I'm incredibly thankful for the accountability relationships the Lord's given me along the way. Who knows how my relationship with my wife and children would have turned out if I hadn't "fallen on the rock" and Alan and Mike weren't there to help me make adjustments in my family life and marriage? Where would I be spiritually and how developed would my leadership skills be if I didn't have accountability relationships with key mentors and leaders along the way? Clearly, my life would be very different indeed!

It is only by intentionally developing strong accountability relationships that we can create the relational mirrors in our lives needed to show us our chalky white "toothpaste" moments, and help us make the changes we need to become the person and live the life God intended for us.

POINTS TO PONDER

1. Who are the people in your life you've invited to hold you accountable in areas of spiritual growth and integrity?

2. Are you listening to their advice/correction and remaining open to their instruction?

3. Are you truly walking in biblical accountability or is it happening in name only?

PRAYER

"Dear Lord, I thank You for intending us to have strong accountability relationships so we never have to walk alone in life. I ask You to please guide and direct me into strong and healthy relationships that are both enjoyable and mutually beneficial, where we can together strengthen and encourage each other. Please forgive me for the times I've been too proud to seek such help and I ask You to help me walk humbly and honestly with those You place in my life. Thank You that ultimately You are the third cord that adds immeasurable strength and blessing to any of my relationships. In Jesus' name. Amen."

17

KING OF THE ROAD:
The God of Above & Beyond

THE SUN MIXED WITH THE RUSHING AIR AND BATHED MY face in warmth as I rounded the curve and began ascending the next hill. I felt the strong pull of the bike beneath me as the 96-cubic inch motor (nearly 1600 cc) bore down to make the climb. Douglas Firs lined the roadway, their distinctive green framing the lushness of the surrounding fields and valleys. In the distance, suddenly rising above the rolling foothills like alert sentinels, was the imposing bluish-grey outline of the Rocky Mountains. I could smell the scent of pine and occasionally the aroma of freshly cut hay or sweet alfalfa.

Ah yes, I thought. *I love riding my motorcycle! It truly is one of life's great pleasures! And, I'm so blessed to have the foothills so close to home. Just a twenty-minute ride and I'm in the middle of all this beauty!* This could describe any one of a number of privileged occasions I've had since moving to Calgary, Alberta in 2011. The city of 1.2 million (and counting) is blessed to be so close to the foothills and Rockies.

None of this would be possible, however, if it weren't for a significant event in 2009. In the spring of that year, my situation was hopeless when it came to motorcycle riding; I had no training, no motorcycle, and most importantly, no agreement from my wife that I could ever become a rider. Some of our friends at The Bridge in Medicine Hat, the church we were leading at the time, started purchasing bikes and sharing their stories. I began to get the itch. A couple of times I mentioned during my Sunday morning message that I'd love to ride a bike someday. Both times, Valerie sat in the front row slowly shaking her head—definitely not a good sign.

Finally, my big break came. After our citywide Good Friday service, a young man from our church, Nathan, approached me with a proposal. "Ian," he said, "would you like to learn to ride a motorcycle?" The question seemed to come out of left field and yet I was already primed with the answer.

"Definitely," I said with enthusiasm.

"I have two motorcycles," Nathan continued, "and so you could learn on one of them and we could ride together." The plan was getting better by the second. "All you need to do is purchase some riding gear and we're ready to go!"

This is fantastic! I thought. *The biggest expense is the bike and that's already taken care of. Compared to that, finding some equipment is a cinch.* "I'm in," I concluded and shook Nathan's hand with a big grin on my face.

My biggest hurdle would be convincing Val this was a good thing. My brothers-in-law, however, were already helping me overcome that obstacle. They had shown a sudden interest in motorcycle riding and all three of them had recently purchased bikes—with their wives' approval. The positive peer pressure was a good thing and Val begrudgingly agreed.

I immediately found deals on a helmet, gloves, riding boots, and a leather jacket. Now I was all ready to go and was greatly anticipating my first lesson. The wait was longer than expected, however, as we had difficulty synchronizing our schedules. April turned to May, became June, and then July. Finally, in August we found a suitable riding time for early September.

In the meantime, my brothers-in-law were regularly riding together and enjoying the good life. At an August family reunion, as we huddled in the backyard swapping stories, my brother-in-law

Les turned and said to me, "When are you going to get a motorcycle? You got the rest of us all excited about it and now you don't even have one yourself."

After Nathan's offer to teach me I'd become a bit of a biker evangelist, zealously sharing my riding plans with others. As I stood there at the reunion, I really wished I could tell Les I'd be getting one soon, but alas, that wasn't the case. "Val and I've talked about it and we don't see it in our budget for the foreseeable future," I said quietly.

It was sad but true. We just couldn't imagine a way to purchase a motorcycle, no matter how great a diversion or stress relief it might represent from my regular ministry functions. Other riding pastors from my city told me how refreshing it was to hop on their bikes and take a short ride to blow off steam and escape the pressures of the day. I was somewhat envious (in a very Christian sort of way) but knew for the moment it wasn't meant to be; our oldest son was going into university in the fall and our other three also had pressing needs.

Once I faced this reality, I remember putting it all into God's hands. I prayed something like, "Lord, if having this as a hobby is going to be beneficial to my mental and emotional wellbeing, and if it's Your will for me to do this, then You're going to have to give me a motorcycle. Amen." That was it. I'm not sure that even really counts as a prayer. Anyway, I prayed once and then promptly forgot about it. I didn't put a picture on the fridge to remind me to regularly pray (although there's nothing wrong with doing so if that's what the Lord directs). I just let it go.

In September, my first lesson was in the parking lot of the abandoned Wal-Mart (the new Supercentre had been open less than a year). Around and around I rode, learning to shift and manoeuver at slow speeds on Nathan's bike—a Harley-Davidson Heritage Softail Classic. I remember marveling at the bike's incredible handling ability and its stunning appearance. My brother-in-law Art once told me there were only two colors for a Harley—black and chrome—and this bike definitely validated that adage.

After the lesson, I asked Nathan to join me at Starbucks for a drink. It was a beautiful late summer's day and perfect for one last visit under a green and white umbrella with a cool frappa-something in our hands. As we sat sipping our drinks and chatting, little did I know I was about to enter my motorcycle destiny. Within minutes, the wife of a good friend of mine (who lived in another city) walked out the coffee shop door and noticed Nathan and me sitting there. After exchanging pleasantries, I told her Nathan was teaching me to ride and pointed to his bike sitting in the parking lot. To be honest, I don't remember specifically what else I said, but judging from the results of the conversation, it's obvious I told her I didn't own a motorcycle.

Nearly two weeks later I was in another city, and amazingly, ran into the same lady and her husband. As we chatted he said to me, "My wife told me you're learning to ride a motorcycle." I nodded. "Have you purchased one yet?" As with Les, I explained it just wasn't in our budget. That's when he dropped the bombshell. "Ian," he said, "I've been trying to contact you and tell you I've decided to give you my motorcycle. I sensed God wanted me to give it away to someone and I've been praying about who that should be. I believe it's you. It's a very nice bike and I think you'll really like it!"

At that point, it really didn't matter how old or in what condition the motorcycle was. All I could think was, *he wants to GIVE me his motorcycle. Free. Wow, what an answer to prayer!* My excitement ramped up as he explained the bike was a Heritage Softail Classic. That's when my jaw hit the floor as I thought, *A Heritage—just like Nathan's! He's GIVING me a $20,000 motorcycle! Can this be for real?* You see, I would have been very pleased with an older motorcycle worth $2,000—even if it burned blue smoke and looked like it was a reject from one of Evel Knievel's failed jumps—as long as it worked. After all, beggars can't be choosers and anything would have been an answer to my prayer. But no, the bike was a Heritage Softail Classic with 3,000 km on it—a Cadillac of motorcycles. How cool was that!!

I was stunned and didn't know how to respond. Saying "thank you" profusely really only goes so far. How do you let someone know the true magnitude of your appreciation for such an amazing gift? Regardless, we arranged for me to pick up the bike at a later date and I said goodbye. *How will I explain this to Val or anyone else for that matter,* I wondered.

Beyond the obvious blessing of having a beautiful motorcycle to ride, the Harley gift spoke volumes about God's immense love for me, His child, and His limitless ability to answer prayer. Who could conceive that a short prayer and a drink at Starbucks could be the catalyst for such an amazing opportunity? It's like a moment in our journey when our life highway suddenly rounds a corner, and unexpectedly, we encounter a breathtaking vista that's unimaginably beautiful. We were just rolling along through the ordinary terrain of daily life, and then, incredibly, everything changed.

A Scripture passage comes to mind exemplifying how God creates such sudden transformations. Ephesians 3 verses 20–21 says, *"Now to him who is able to do immeasurably more than all we ask or imagine, according to his power that is at work within us, to him be glory in the church and in Christ Jesus throughout all generations, for ever and ever! Amen."* These two verses come at the end of a powerful prayer by Paul the Apostle as he asks God to strengthen the Ephesian church and help them come to a full understanding of the immenseness of His great love for them. (If you haven't read it lately, I encourage you to do so.) It's as if he's putting an exclamation on this powerful intercession by declaring God can do immeasurably more than even the greatest plans our puny minds can devise!

I asked the Lord for a motorcycle and He responded by doing far more than I ever imagined. He didn't just give me any bike, but rather an expensive Harley Davidson that will provide much enjoyment for Val and me in the years ahead. Initially, I struggled with the extravagance of the gift and felt completely unworthy. *This is over the top,* I thought. *I don't deserve this!* But then it was like hearing the Lord's still small voice reassuring me inside—as if He were saying, "It's alright, Ian. I want you to enjoy the motorcycle. Your father died when you were twelve and his absence meant you couldn't do some of the fun things like other boys your age. I want you to regain that now. I want you to have fun with this. Receive it as a gift from your heavenly Father who greatly loves you. Enjoy!" Jesus used parables to convey truth, and for me, the gift of this motorcycle has become a living parable, pointing me to a God who can do *"immeasurably more than we can ask or imagine."*

I received the motorcycle in the fall of 2009, just before we embarked on our year-long transition from ministry in Medicine Hat and began our Calgary church-planting journey in 2011. I don't believe that was a coincidence, as I sensed the "above and beyond" nature of the gift was also encouraging me to believe for *over-the-top* results in Calgary. I needed a big and extravagant dream about what God could do through our church in that city of over a million people.

Likewise, all of us need great expectations and dreams no matter what God is calling us to do. Someone unafraid to do this is Tommy Barnett, co-pastor with son Luke, of the 20,000-member congregation in Phoenix, Arizona, now known as Dream City Church. Pastor Tommy also started the Los Angeles Dream Centre with his son Matthew, illustrating that he knows a thing or two about dreaming big and following God's extravagant purposes for one's life.

"Dreams ... are the goals and visions that fire your heart and saturate your soul with joy at the very thought of them," writes Pastor Tommy. "They are those continuing visions of what you want your life to be at its highest level of fulfillment—what you want to do, how you want to do it, what kind of person you want to become in the process. . . A dream doesn't drive you; it draws you. It is like a big magnet that pulls you toward itself."[1]

The question, however, is how do we cultivate such dreams and lift our sights higher so this *magnet* can begin to pull us along? Thankfully, Pastor Tommy has shared some very practical steps for doing this in his article, *Are You Dreaming BIG Enough.*[2]

The first priority is getting alone and spending time with the Father. Psalm 46:10 tells us to *"Be still and know that I am God."* If I really want to get serious about hearing from the Lord, I must get away for a night or two on a personal retreat. Just leaving familiar surroundings, including the TV and other distractions, helps clear my mind and spirit and prepares me to receive fresh revelation from Him.

Like Paul the Apostle, who spent years in the desert listening to the Lord before he began his ministry, we need to ask God to identify the overarching, all-consuming passion that we'll pursue until we die. Once we discover that, we can let it direct our steps and focus.

During the first few months after we left Medicine Hat, I vividly recall spending much time praying for Church of the Rock Calgary's vision. What was God's big dream for this church and His great purpose behind it being established in our city? Understanding that was key to us launching in January 2012.

After seeking God, we next need to consider our gifts and talents, as previously indicated. God has designed us a certain way, for a certain purpose. Consequently, we will never be completely fulfilled unless we embrace that unique design and seek to live out that divine purpose. In essence, our unique giftings point us toward God's will and dream for our lives.

I'll never forget a humorous illustration used by Ken Malmin, one of my favorite teachers at Portland Bible College in the early 80s. To highlight the importance of us functioning according to our individual giftings, he imagined what would happen if a can opener began to envy the work and function of a toaster. He painted the picture of the can opener deciding to mimic the toaster's function but instead shredding the bread as it rotated round and round. It's a strange picture, but one that's stayed with me for more than thirty years. Since we're each unique and made by God for a specific purpose, it's pointless and even harmful (just think of the bread) to try to mimic the calling and function of others. It's therefore vital we properly assess our gifts and abilities and then "stay in our lane," as it were. (Review chapter 14 for more information and a free assessment process).

Val and I had a God-given dream to start a new church here in Calgary, but it would have been foolish to pursue if we didn't have the proper gifts and abilities required. For the sake of full disclosure, I didn't actually take any church planting assessment tests prior to our new church launching—we weren't aware of that process at the time. I filled one out after we'd started, however, and was incredibly relieved to find out that, yes, I did indeed have the skills to start a new church. What would we have done at that point if I didn't? Scary indeed! Ultimately, we're just asking for frustration and failure when we try to pursue a dream without the proper gifting and abilities.

Once we consider our gifts and talents, we must give thought to our life experiences to see how God can use even the bad ones in our life—such as divorce, alcoholism, or bankruptcy—to provide the underpinnings of fulfilling our destiny. The trials Val and I experienced with so much loss at a relatively young age—the death of my father when I was 12 and the loss of her parents when she was 19 and I was 20—have made us stronger and more resilient, which helped us in church leadership and starting a new work. Ultimately, we believe the Lord is using the grief of our past to assist with producing new life and transformation in the lives of others today.

Next, once you're clear on your abilities and experiences, it's important to establish specific goals and a clear focus, and begin exploring different avenues to fulfill your dream—not giving attention to those nonessentials that won't matter ten years from now. More and more I'm discovering I must give up activities that are merely good, so I can concentrate my focus on those areas which will produce great fruit for God's Kingdom. Writing this book is a prime example of such focus. I sensed God's call to complete this manuscript, but it was only possible when I narrowed my focus, gave up other activities, and determined to persevere until I accomplished the goal.

Finally, after spending time with God, considering gifts and talents, giving thought to life experiences, and establishing clear goals and focus, it's essential to write the vision down. Habakkuk 2:2 says, *"Then the Lord answered me and said: 'Write the vision and make it plain on tablets, that he may run who reads it'"* (NKJV). This brings clarity and helps you move the dream forward by taking specific pre-determined steps. Otherwise, a God-given vision can just degenerate into wishful thinking. Before launching COTR Calgary, for example, it was vital we established and clearly articulated our vision, mission, and values, so the focus and direction of our church would always remain clear and intentional. Today, we're committed to "Introducing God's transforming love into your life, our community, and the world—because He first loved us," and we assess everything we do based upon the fulfillment of this vision.

Once we've done our part to seek the Lord and walk through a process of determining His great dream for our lives, we need to rely on His awesome ability to do those things that are *"above and beyond all that we can ask or even imagine."* The Psalmist said, *"Trust in the Lord and do good. Then you will live safely in the land and prosper. Take delight in the Lord and he will give you your heart's desires. Commit everything you do to the Lord. Trust him, and he will help you"* (Psalm 37:3–5 NLT).

What are you asking God to do in and through your life? Are your imaginations great enough or are you still hoping just to survive? Do you believe the Lord can exceed your expectations and bless you, or are you still living in the disappointments of the past? It may be time to ask forgiveness for thinking and believing too small, and instead, open yourself up again to the God who can *"do immeasurably more than all we ask or imagine, according to His power that is at work within us*"—to the God who provides a Harley Davidson motorcycle to one of His sons, just because He can … and because it pleases Him!

POINTS TO PONDER

1. What is your plan to take time to get alone with God, hear His voice, and begin receiving His vision for your life?

2. What are the gifts and talents God has given you? How can you begin activating them?

3. What are the unique experiences in your life, even the bad ones, that could provide the foundation for God to fulfill your destiny?

4. What are the important priorities on which you should focus so you can begin pursuing your God-given dreams?

5. What is the essence of the vision you sense God has for your life?

6. Do you need to ask God to forgive you for thinking and believing too small about what He can do in your life? Is there anything else hindering God from doing "above and beyond" in your life?

PRAYER

"Dear Lord, I thank You for loving me and having great plans for my life. Nothing is too hard for You and I repent of the times I haven't believed this. I ask You now to help me pick up my big dreams and believe again that You can fulfill them—because You're a big God with unlimited power. I'm so thankful You can "do immeasurably more than all we ask or imagine" according to Your power "that is at work within us." Amen."

TRANSPORTING GOD'S BLESSINGS:
Living with Eternity in Mind

ONE SUMMER WHILE VACATIONING IN BONNER'S FERRY, Idaho, Val and I toured the local museum to learn more about the region's history and famous citizens. It was fascinating to see an early 20ᵗʰ century bedroom, for example, complete with an ornate Victorian style bed and dresser. One area of the museum showcased the interior of the original post office, while another recreated one of the town's famous bars—complete with a life-size standup photograph of the owner standing behind the counter.

As we strode through the complex, we marveled at the great variety of displays and the preserved period photographs highlighting the early days of pioneering. Near the end of the tour, we entered a room with forty commissioned oil portraits of some of the area's past leaders in business, education, and politics including the longtime local pharmacist, past aboriginal tribe leaders, school teachers, mayors, nurses, and doctors.

Immediately adjacent to this *wall of fame* were some impressive displays; one was of finely handcrafted and intricately designed clocks, including one that looked like the Eiffel tower. The maker, a longtime area resident, had spent countless hours on each one, with some having more than 1,000 unique pieces individually cut on a scroll saw. Beside that collection was another of handmade wooden toys, such as a finely crafted train, logging truck, tractor, and combine. Their creator took pride in paying great attention to detail—making sure, for example, that the fire truck ladders swung and functioned properly, tracks on the bulldozer and excavator turned on their handmade pads, and the pitch and swing of the road grader were authentic. I marveled at these creations and admired the incredible skill and industriousness of the craftsmen.

As I left the museum, however, I was struck with life's brevity. Many of those celebrated by the displays, photographs, and portraits were long gone from this world, taking with them their wisdom, skills and abilities, but leaving behind all of their accomplishments. King Solomon, whom some think was the wisest man who ever lived, wrote about how he viewed this:

> I hated all the things I had toiled for under the sun, because I must leave them to the one who comes after me. And who knows whether he will be a wise man or a fool? Yet he will have control over all the work into which I have poured my effort and skill under the sun. This too is meaningless ... For a man may do his work with wisdom, knowledge and skill, and then he must leave all he owns to someone who has not worked for it. This too is meaningless and a great misfortune (Ecclesiastes 2:18–21 NIV84).

At the end of his life, as Solomon surveyed the landscape of his existence, he lamented the conclusion.

Job, one of the most prosperous men of his time, writes: *"Naked I came from my mother's womb, and naked I will depart"* (Job 1:21). As someone once said of our earthly belongings, "You can't take them with you, and I've never seen a U-Haul follow a hearse to the gravesite."

Like Solomon, the key question after my day at the museum was, "What truly is a lasting legacy?" All the *stuff* we create here on earth eventually decays and is forgotten. What can we do that will make a difference and be remembered forever? Someone who genuinely understood the answer to this question was Jean Byrd, my mother. At the end of her life, she died with little money and a small life insurance policy, but she left a priceless legacy with her family and all those she touched in her years of pastoring.

My mother was a generous woman and ultimately a great example of how to live a Christ-like life. God wants us to properly use what He's provided so our lives become a highway which will transport His blessings and provision to others. Whenever my mother received some unexpected money above and beyond her basic living, she would always tithe ten percent and then give generously above that. Sometimes I would express my concerns she was giving away too much, considering her personal needs. However, she would always reply, "Ian, I'm storing up treasures in Heaven," a reference to the passage in Matthew where it says:

> "Do not store up for yourselves treasure on earth, where moth and rust destroy, and where thieves break in and steal. But store up for yourselves treasures in heaven, where moth and rust do not destroy, and where thieves do not break in and steal. For where your treasure is, there your heart will be also (Matthew 6:19–21 NIV84).

I've often heard that if we are to be successful and achieve our goals, we need to start with the end in mind. That's exactly what my mother was doing. She wanted to make sure when she curved up the mountain, rounded her last turn in life, and saw the Lord for the first time (as with the picture in Psalm 84:7 MSG), there were treasures and rewards sent ahead to make her eternal stay more enjoyable. To ensure this happened, she regularly reminded herself of this truth and then looked for opportunities to give and to bless.

The treasure she sent ahead for storage wasn't just money, either. It was also the investing of her time and God-given talents to make a difference in the lives of others. Like her, we must always consider: *Am I effectively using my time, talents, and finances to honor God and build His Kingdom and thereby storing treasure in Heaven?*

Randy Alcorn, author of *The Treasure Principle* sums it up well: "I think of our lives in terms of a dot and a line, signifying two phases. Our present life on earth is the dot. It begins. It ends. It's brief. However, from the dot, a line extends that goes on forever. That line is eternity, which Christians will spend in heaven. Right now we're living in the dot. But what are we living for? The short-sighted person lives for the dot. The person with perspective lives for the line."[1]

Author John Surowiecki concurs when he writes, "Of the various kinds of intelligence, generosity is the first."[2]

I vividly remember God correcting me for not having such a generous, intelligent mindset; one that would store up treasures in Heaven. I was in my early 30's with a young family and running a small business. We had two vehicles, a 1987 Dodge Caravan for Val and the boys, and a 1987 Ford Tempo I used for work. Our church had small groups meeting in members' homes, and one week Frank Amantea, a good friend of ours, was visiting our church and decided to share with our group about his mission work in the Philippines.

As he talked about his family's needs, he mentioned they were raising money to purchase a greatly needed Jeepney—a bus-like vehicle unique to the Philippines. The minute he mentioned his goal, I sensed the Lord prompting me to sell my Ford Tempo and give the proceeds to Frank for the new vehicle—an amount likely to be $2,000. It certainly wasn't an audible voice, but an impression in my heart. I'd love to say I was so obedient I immediately listed my vehicle in the newspaper classifieds and had it sold in a week. I'd love to say that, but I can't. Instead, I mulled it over for a few days.

Was that really God? I questioned. *After all, I still need a vehicle for my personal use while Val uses the van to transport the boys. That couldn't be God. He knows I really need the Tempo. It must have been some random thought.* I knew that still small inner voice because I'd heard it before and deep down I was fairly confident

God had spoken to me. I once heard someone say they had the urge to work but then they laid down until that feeling went away. That's what I did with the impression at the small group. I pushed it aside and refused to listen until finally, it went away, taking with it my opportunity to be used as a blessing on Earth, and to send some treasure on ahead to Heaven.

I thought that was the end of it, but then I sensed God speak to me in an even more direct manner and I didn't like what I heard. Some claim to have heard God speak to them audibly. That's never happened to me, but what occurred next was close enough.

One day I was walking through the hallway of our house and had just turned into the bathroom when almost audibly I heard this phrase, "You are so minimal in your giving!" I knew it was the Lord and I also knew it was a judgment about the way I was living. It was like God had been observing my behavior and how reticent I was to be generous and assist others. He'd given me a chance to honor Him in my giving, but I'd disobeyed.

Now, like the gavel being dropped by the judge, He was declaring His verdict and that meant He was determined to do something about my selfish and stingy attitude. He loved me too much to let me remain in a place where I wasn't effectively being a conduit of His blessing to a hurting and needy world. He also loved me too much to let me remain in a place where He couldn't truly bless me. When we give to others, God is able to give back to us *"pressed down, shaken together and running over"* (Luke 6:38).

Because He wanted my heart to shift into a position of generosity which would enable me to leave a true, lasting legacy, circumstances soon came that challenged me financially and caused me to realize God was my source and everything I had was His. He was the owner; I was merely the manager. This being the case, when He asked me to steward His resources to help and benefit others, I needed to quickly obey.

The financial struggles I endured during the next few years (as I started and then had to shut down a publishing business) showed the onset of this learning process. This was followed by a marketing sales position and eventually work as a straight commission investment consultant with no base salary. That season of hand-to-mouth living definitely taught me man *"shall not live on bread alone, but on every Word that comes from the mouth of God"* (Matthew 4:4).

At the end of that time, something had indeed shifted in my heart and I was much more generous and open to giving to others; eternity now took the forefront of my thoughts and behaviors, and material possessions finally took a back seat. I became pastor of the church in Medicine Hat and my life also became more financially consistent.

Then, in the summer of 2007, the Lord decided to retest me with the same request He presented twelve years earlier. One day as I sat in my church office, the phone suddenly rang. It was Val on the other end who proceeded to tell me how she'd just talked to a young mom in our church whose van had broken down. The woman and her husband were praying about what to do next, as they didn't have the money to purchase a new vehicle.

"So," Val said, "I was thinking we should maybe give them our van. What do you think?"

In a split second, several thoughts went through my head. *I like our van. It's eleven years old, but it's still in great shape. We could still use it for a few years and so we should keep it.* However, that was quickly followed by, *But what is God saying? Is this an impression Val's receiving from Him? Is He asking us to sacrificially give our van away and trust Him for something else? I mean, we do have four sons, so if we give away the van how will we travel together? That will be so inconvenient ... however, if He's truly asking us to do this, He'll provide a way. Plus, I don't want to be disobedient like I was in the 90s when He asked me to sell the Tempo—that didn't turn out so well!*

The pros and cons bounced around in my head like a high-speed ping-pong game, but finally, I came to peace in my heart when I determined we should step out in faith and give away the van. God's eternal plan, I believed, trumped the inconveniences this situation would present—and whether or not others understood, or merely thought we were crazy.

"I think we should do it," I concluded.

"Really?" Val said. "You're sensing that too?"

"Yes," I said. "I agree God wants us to give the van to this young family!"

After hanging up I had this strange excitement in my spirit. The van was worth about $4,000, but I knew God would eventually provide another vehicle. In the meantime, we'd somehow manage. It felt good to know we were trusting the Lord and willing to participate in His adventure.

A couple of days later, we had the privilege of escorting the young family into our garage. Motioning to the purple Grand Caravan I said, "It's all yours!" With dumbfounded faces, they looked at us and the young mother said, "Really? Are you sure?"

"Yes," we stated emphatically. "We want you to have this vehicle."

"But what will you guys do to transport your family?" she protested.

"Don't worry about that," I said. "We're confident God has a plan."

With that, we handed over the keys, said a prayer of blessing upon them and their new vehicle, and watched as they and their three kids piled into the van and drove off. Their children were seeing firsthand how God provides for our needs, while ours were learning that living with an eternal focus sometimes means sacrifice and making inconvenient decisions.

Thankfully, someone in our church became aware we were now vanless and said we could drive a late model Dodge Acclaim they had bought for their daughter who would turn 16 in a year. In the meantime, they were pleased for us to have its use. For a time, whenever all six of us went somewhere we had to take my 2001

Honda Accord and the Dodge Acclaim. At first, the whole situation was like a fresh adventure, but then as time wore on it began getting a bit old as we continued jockeying between two vehicles.

One day as I began having negative second thoughts about our decision to give away the van, the Lord provided insight that's helped me deal with such difficulties ever since. In my spirit, I heard Him say, "Inconvenience is worship!" As I considered that phrase, I came to understand what He meant. Every time a choice to sacrificially obey God results in things getting harder and our lifestyle being inconvenienced, that becomes an act of worship—provided we keep a good attitude. Therefore, as we drove around in the late model Acclaim, we chose to thank the Lord for His provision and also be grateful for the opportunity to obey and serve Him.

Soon the Lord provided a solution. Good friends of ours sensed God telling them to give us their 2001 Dodge Grand Caravan. It was humbling but also very exciting to sense our time of two-vehicle travel was finally coming to a close. We gratefully picked up the van from its owners and drove to church as a family the next Sunday.

After concluding the service, I headed to the parking lot to hop in the van and go home. On the way to our parking stall, however, I suddenly noticed the van of one of our church members. The driver front fender of his late model Grand Caravan was falling off and other parts of the vehicle definitely looked worse for wear. I knew the van was very important to his small business and I had a sudden surge of compassion for his situation. It was then I heard that now familiar small voice say, *"Want to go again?"* I knew what that meant. The Lord was offering us another opportunity to give away yet another vehicle and continue our faith adventure with him.

When I reached the white Grand Caravan, I said to Val, "I think the Lord wants us to give away this vehicle too." I motioned to our friend's vehicle and told her I thought he should be the recipient.

She quickly nodded her approval because she had also noticed his need and sensed we were supposed to act … we gave away that van too. For the next fourteen months, we returned to the dual vehicle solution until the Lord encouraged some good friends to sell us their Pontiac Montana van at an excellent price.

When we freely give of our time, talents, along with our treasure, we're intentionally living with eternity in mind and actively working to create a legacy superseding our earthly lives—something far more precious and valuable than the stuff we accumulate. Paul the Apostle addresses this issue in his first letter to the church in Corinth. He starts by reminding them the foundation of their lives is their relationship with Jesus Christ. He then provides specific instructions on how to build so as to serve and live for Him.

> *If anyone builds on this foundation using gold, silver, costly stones, wood, hay or straw, their work will be shown for what it is, because the Day will bring it to light. It will be revealed with fire, and the fire will test the quality of each person's work. If what has been built survives, the builder will receive a reward. If it is burned up, the builder will suffer loss but yet will be saved—even though only as one escaping through the flames* (1 Corinthians 3:12–15).

Paul is painting a vivid picture of the day when all believers will stand before Christ and give an account for their earthly lives (Romans 14:10–12). If the substance of their existence was merely the accumulation of wealth and worldly treasure, it will not survive divine scrutiny but will burn up into ashes. They will still enter Heaven since they received Jesus as Savior and are forgiven of their sins, but it will seem as though they have lost everything—like a family barely escaping a house fire with just the clothes on their backs. However, those who spent their earthly time, talents and treasure on building God's Kingdom and obediently investing in the lives of others will have a great reward. They are the ones who will receive the commendation, "Well done good and faithful servant!" (Matthew 25:21).

The key to keeping our mind off of selfish pursuits and the mere accumulation of possessions is to focus on what truly matters. Again, Paul addresses this perfectly in his second letter to the church at Corinth: *"For our light and momentary troubles are achieving for us an eternal glory that far outweighs them all. So we fix our eyes not on what is seen, but on what is unseen, since what is seen is temporary, but what is unseen is eternal"* (2 Corinthians 4:17–18).

Paul encourages the Corinthians to look past their current difficulties and instead see the eternal reward waiting for them because of their obedience and sacrifice. In comparison to the glory of that reward, those sacrifices—no matter how great—are actually "light" and "momentary." Likewise, our eternal legacy far outweighs whatever inconvenience or discomfort our steps of obedience may cause throughout our years on earth. This legacy doesn't just await us in Heaven but hopefully will be reproduced in the earthly lives of others who witness our journey—our church family, friends, and most of all, our own children.

And, as if an eternal and residual reward in Heaven weren't enough, Jesus said we would eventually receive blessing here on Earth for our Kingdom sacrifices. His statement is in response to His most outspoken disciple, Peter, who asks a question all Christ-followers have probably had (or at least thought) at one time or another: *"We have left everything to follow you! What then will there be for us?"* (Matthew 19:27). In other words, we twelve disciples have really sacrificed to obey and follow You, so how will we be compensated for our special devotion? Jesus' response should be a great encouragement and motivation to us all: *"Truly I tell you … no one who has left home or wife or brothers or sisters or parents or children for the sake of the kingdom of God will fail to receive many times as much in this age, and in the age to come eternal life"* (Luke 18:29).

Even though this is a specific response to the twelve disciples, Jesus extends it to all who have ever sacrificed materially or relationally for His sake—and He declares they will receive "many times as much"—a great return on investment!

Although the tremendous magnitude of our eternal reward should be, in itself, our primary motivation, it's great to also know we can expect God to bless and provide for our needs now, even as we become conduits of His grace and blessing to a hurting world (Philippians 4:19). I conclude by leaving you with one question: *"What are you investing in and are you creating a lasting legacy with eternity in mind?"*

POINTS TO PONDER

1. What time, talent, or treasures is the Lord asking you to give to His service? What steps can you take to begin obeying His call? What is hindering you from doing so?

2. How generous are you? Are there times God has asked you to give and serve others, but you've waited until the feeling went away?

3. Are you living for the dot, or for the line? How can you regularly remind yourself of the eternal importance of the line?

PRAYER

"Dear God, I thank You for the many ways You bless and provide for my every need. All I have comes from You. As You are generous with me, please help me to likewise use my time, talents, and treasure to bless others and build Your Kingdom. I want to live for the line and create a lasting legacy, and so I ask You to daily help me remember eternity. In Jesus' name. Amen."

19

ROUNDING THE FINAL CURVE:
Leaving a Lasting Legacy

"God-traveled, these roads curve up the mountain,
and at the last turn—Zion! God in full view!"
Psalm 84:7, MSG)

ENTERING THE INTENSIVE CARE UNIT, I HURRIED TO THE reception desk. "Which room is Jean Byrd in?" I inquired of the nurse while trying to stay calm. The young woman pointed just a short distance down the hall. "Thank you," I said as Val and I briskly walked to the glass-enclosed cubicle where an attendant sat just outside, monitoring my mother's oxygen levels, heart rate, and other vitals.

It was less than twenty-four hours since the hospital first called to inform us Mom had been brought there by ambulance. I was in my home office finalizing the layout for the next edition of my television magazine, so Val volunteered to make the half hour drive to Lethbridge and assist her. It was three years since my mother's first stroke, soon after her 65th birthday—a relatively minor one that nevertheless reduced her motor skills on her right side so she walked with a limp and had reduced use of that arm. Unfortunately, however, that was just the start of a series of strokes that continued to diminish her mobility. What followed were frequent hospital stays, a move from her basement suite to a senior's apartment and then one to an assisted living lodge. At times, she would stay with our family to recuperate. This reoccurring cycle made us confident the Sunday evening's episode would end up just being another temporary stay, and we weren't too panicked by the situation.

Later that night, Val called to tell me Mom was looking pretty good and had even signed herself into the hospital. Apparently, the aids at the lodge were not sure what had happened but thought she maybe had had another stroke.

Well, it doesn't sound too bad, I thought. *If she could sign herself in then she'll probably just be in overnight for observation and then quickly back to the seniors' lodge.*

That prognosis changed, however, at 10 a.m. the next morning. The hospital called and the nurse on the line had grim news. "It's likely your mother had a stroke yesterday and then aspirated," she began. "As a result, she now has pneumonia and is fading fast. You need to get in here quickly, as she may not last the day."

After recovering from initial shock, we quickly followed the nurse's advice and I now stood at my mother's bedside. She was fully awake but couldn't speak because of a tube down her throat clearing fluid from her lungs. The steady flow of black liquid, however, made me realize the situation was dire. After saying hello, I sensed the Lord prompt me it was also time to say goodbye. At first, I struggled with that impression but then made a decision that even if this wasn't Mom's time to depart for Heaven, expressing my love and thankfulness to her for being a good mother was never a bad thing.

Clearing my throat, I said, "Mom, I want to thank you for all the sacrifices you made for me and Peter after dad died. It wasn't easy raising two boys on your own, but you did it so well and gave us a great example of how important it is to love and serve the Lord with our whole hearts."

Her smile quickly disappeared, her eyes became somewhat defiant and her forehead creased. Her face was saying, *Don't you dare do this now. I'm not going to die!*

I pushed back, however. "No, Mom, I must say this. You need to hear how proud I am of you and how thankful for the excellent mother you are."

At this she relented and tears filled her eyes. I kissed her on the cheek and then prayed the Lord would heal and restore her. This was the last contact I would have with her in this life, as later in the day they sedated my mother and she never regained consciousness.

At 2 a.m. the following morning, October 31st, 1996, as Val and I stood by her bedside and I told her, "Just go home to be with Jesus," my mother passed away at the age of 68. At the relatively young age of 31, both my and Val's parents were now in Heaven.

I have only one regret from that evening; that I didn't ask Mom to say hello to Dad for me! After all, how many people do you meet that are imminently heading to Heaven and could carry such a greeting? Sheesh!

That night, Earth's loss was Heaven's gain. Along with her role as a loving wife and mother, my beautiful, vivacious, red-haired mom was an incredibly loyal friend to many, and one of the most caring, conscientious and inspiring pastors you would ever meet— serving four small churches while raising her two teenage sons as a single mother. To this day, she's my hero! She was so inspirational and life-giving that after her retirement at 55, one of the local funeral homes still hired her to officiate when they had a family with no pastoral connection. Her beautiful smile, laughing eyes, and effusive personality brought light and warmth to even the saddest occasion.

For all of us there will be a time when, like my mother, our life highways will come to an end, and *"God-traveled, these roads curve up the mountain, and at the last turn—Zion! God in full view!"* (Psalm 84:7 MSG). Those of us who, like her, have put our hope in the salvation of Jesus Christ and served His purposes during our days here on Earth, will breathe our last and in the next instant be with the Lord in Heaven.

The thought of this is both exhilarating and sobering to me all at the same time. Seeing my Savior face to face will be wonderful, but it's another matter to stand before Him and answer for my life as the Bible states we all will do (Romans 14:12). That level of accountability for my actions and every careless word I've spoken (Matthew 12:36) strikes the fear of God into me. It causes me to realize that, like my mother, I should be living in a manner the Lord can reward and applaud later. I've frequently heard effective planning starts with having the end in mind. That's certainly true when it comes to our entire existence. The question we all must ask is, "What is the type of life I want to answer for when I stand before God? What is the legacy I wish to leave?"

I can think of only one answer to that question: Like my mother, I want to live an inspiring life that ultimately points others toward a personal relationship with Jesus Christ. This includes how we treat people and the kind things we do for them in the name of Christ. The Bible is clear this type of activity will be greatly rewarded. In the book of Matthew, Jesus describes what will happen when He returns. Everyone will be gathered around Him; He will separate the sheep from the goats—the believer from nonbeliever, and each one will be dealt with accordingly:

> *"Then the King will say to those on his right (the believers), 'Come, you who are blessed by my Father; take your inheritance, the kingdom prepared for you since the creation of the world. For I was hungry and you gave me something to eat, I was thirsty and you gave me something to drink, I was a stranger and you invited me in, I needed clothes and you clothed me, I was sick and you looked after me, I was in prison and you came to visit me.' "Then the righteous will answer him, 'Lord, when did we see you hungry and feed you, or thirsty and give you something to drink? When did we see you a stranger and invite you in, or needing clothes and clothe you? When did we see you sick or in prison and go to visit you?'*
>
> *"The King will reply, 'Truly I tell you, whatever you did for*

one of the least of these brothers and sisters of mine, you did for me' (Matthew 25:34–40).

Jesus said when we love and serve others in His name, it's as if we're doing those things directly to Him, and He will reward us accordingly. Imagine ... being *commended* by Him on judgment day! But also imagine, and you will have all of eternity to do so, the impact you had on the people in your sphere of influence. You might have been a link in their coming to know Jesus, and for all eternity their presence will be a reminder of what you did on Earth—true fruit that remains!

Jesus' last words before ascending into Heaven commissioned us to produce such lasting fruit: *"Therefore go and make disciples of all nations, baptizing them in the name of the Father and of the Son and of the Holy Spirit, and teaching them to obey everything I have commanded you. And surely I am with you always, to the very end of the age"* (Matthew 28:19–20).

One of the attitudes often missing in my life and among other Christians today is a sense of urgency about fulfilling this Great Commission and sharing the Good News. Often, we fall into the trap of thinking we'll always have plenty of time to share with others in our lives. Over the years, however, God has used difficult circumstances to show me we can never presume anything about the future. One such occasion occurred in 2001 in Medicine Hat.

During that summer, I worked hard to meet the neighbors who lived on the same street as our church building. Since it was called Dominion Street, I nicknamed the initiative, "Taking Dominion." (Pretty clever, eh?) I began going door-to-door using a questionnaire to quiz people about how we, as a church, could better meet the needs of our community.

Not only did I build a solid relationship with each household, but I also had the privilege of sharing the gospel at a resident's kitchen table and blessing one couple with free yard work as the wife battled against cancer. It truly was an amazing time of making friends and showing the love of Jesus on that street. As a result, I came to know many residents on a first name basis and gained incredible favor for our church.

About mid-summer, we invited a traveling team of young people to visit and assist us in "Taking Dominion" by performing random acts of kindness for street residents such as removing debris and cleaning yards. To prepare for their arrival, I and another leader went door-to-door canvassing homeowners for service opportunities.

We rang the doorbell at one house and an elderly man named Gerry answered. He wasn't looking very healthy, however, and was wearing a mask and guiding an oxygen tank behind him. After explaining the imminent arrival of the youth team, we asked if they could do some yard work for him.

"I have someone taking care of that for me," he said, "so I don't really need the team's help." Looking around at his yard I agreed, as it was well groomed and orderly.

"Would you like to come in?" He suddenly asked, changing the subject.

His imploring eyes and sickly condition tugged at my heart. *This is a very lonely and hurting man,* I thought. My task-oriented tendency kicked in, however, and I remembered we were on a tight schedule—the youth team would be with us soon, and I really needed to get some service assignments booked.

"We can't visit with you today," I said, "but I promise we'll come back soon when we have more time." He nodded and thanked us again for our offer to help, giving us a weak smile before closing the door.

We established some service opportunities, the youth team came and went, and I left on a brief one-week holiday, before finally arriving back on Dominion Street ready to visit Gerry. I hadn't forgotten about him and barely two weeks had passed. I was even taking another church member with me to meet with the ailing man. As I walked toward his house I passed the home of John, whom I had the privilege of getting to know that summer. Sitting on his porch, he asked me where I was going.

"I'm going to visit your neighbor Gerry," I said as I continued on my way.

"He passed away last Thursday," John said. "You won't be visiting him anytime soon."

"What?" I said, stopping in my tracks and turning to face John. He reiterated the sad news and it felt like I'd been punched in the gut. Shock and dismay settled in as I realized I would never have an opportunity to share the Good News about Jesus with Gerry. My fellow church member tried to console me but I was beyond that as tears welled up in my eyes.

He can't be dead! I thought. *I was just here two weeks ago and I kept my promise to come back. God knows I didn't forget! How could he have died in the meantime? Why didn't I visit him when I had the chance? He wanted us to come in; I could see it in his eyes! Why did I delay? What was I thinking?*

I don't know that I've ever really gotten over that mistake. Oh yes, I've asked the Lord to forgive me, and I believe He has, but it's difficult to reconcile with not knowing whether or not Gerry knew Jesus. He might have. Or, he might have needed me to share the truth with him. Now he's in eternity and I can't know for sure!

The lesson learned is that none of us know how long our friends, family, or neighbors have to live on this earth. We need to stop procrastinating, stop making excuses, and begin to take every opportunity to show God's love and share His truth. As the Scriptures say, *"I tell you, now is the time of God's favor, now is the day of salvation!"* (2 Corinthians 6:2 NIV84). Those around us can often look so happy and satisfied we can forget that without Christ they're doomed to an eternity in hell.

Val and I had an experience in Calgary that provides a graphic picture of the tragic condition of most city residents. We were driving home from Sunday service, focused on reaching the restaurant where the rest of our family was planning to meet for lunch. As we headed down a main thoroughfare, we suddenly caught sight of a gaunt, skinny man limping along the sidewalk on the right-hand side of the road. Even more alarming than his halting steps was the waxy yellow appearance of his face. Other than a corpse in a casket, I've never seen a person so deathly pale. His zombie-like appearance was so disturbing that, after briefly losing sight of him, I had to take a second look just to make sure my eyes weren't deceiving me. Val and I drove on in silence as the disturbing image remained vivid in our minds.

In the days following, we repeatedly prayed for the unknown gentleman but also felt challenged, as his condition mirrored the spiritual one of "the walking dead" all around us. If we could view our friends and neighbors through special glasses, I'm sure many of them spiritually look like that man—limping through life in a dazed, trance-like state, spiritually dead and awaiting an eternal dwelling in hell when their body expires. That sounds harsh, but that's reality and God has chosen us to make the difference and be carriers of the Good News, rescuing many from that dark destiny.

In Romans 10:9–13, Paul the Apostle clearly explains this Good News when he writes:

> *If you openly declare that Jesus is Lord and believe in your heart that God raised him from the dead, you will be saved. For it is by believing in your heart that you are made right with God, and it is by openly declaring your faith that you are saved. As the Scriptures tell us, "Anyone who trusts in him will never be disgraced." Jew and Gentile are the same in this respect. They have the same* Lord, *who gives generously to all who call on him. For "Everyone who calls on the name of the* Lord *will be saved"* (NLT).

Beginning in verse 14, Paul goes on to explain our responsibility as bearers of this Gospel:

> *"But how can they call on him to save them unless they believe in him? And how can they believe in him if they have never*

heard about him? And how can they hear about him unless someone tells them? And how will anyone go and tell them without being sent? That is why the Scriptures say, "How beautiful are the feet of messengers who bring good news!" (NLT).

After reading this passage, all Christ followers should make it their goal to have the most beautiful feet in the world as bearers of the Good News. Paul is painting a picture of how vital it is that all of us have a "going" mindset, realizing we've been sent by God to carry this important news. People will not hear the Gospel message unless someone steps out and tells them. We're meant to walk through our world and look for opportunities to share God's salvation message with everyone we meet. Statistics show, however, that this isn't happening like it should.

Sadly, however, there's often a disconnect between what we believe and our actions. We want to share our faith but are hesitant to do so. I think our fear to share with others is often due to a lack of clarity about how to convey that message. We think, *What do I say? What if I get it wrong?* So we do nothing, rather than risk making a mistake.

As a salesman, I spent hours learning my presentation and rehearsing answers to objections; yet, how often do I, and other Christians, prepare to share the greatest presentation in the world? Thankfully, God wanted the Good News to be easily understood by all, so becoming a Christ follower is as simple as **ABC**.

A – Admit we've sinned and fallen short of God's standard of perfection. We're all weak and unable to save ourselves and we need to acknowledge that reality (Romans 3:23).

B – Believe Jesus Christ paid the price for this sin when He died and rose again (1 John 3:8, John 1:12).

C – Confess that we give our lives to Jesus. By making him Lord and Master, we're willing to do whatever He asks while also receiving the forgiveness of all our sins (Romans 10:9–10).

If we can communicate these points in our own words, complete with a few Scriptures to back them up, we'll be well on our way to sharing our faith with others. The key is praying and asking God to help us push through our fear of failure and resist any pride that would keep us from taking the risk of potentially appearing foolish. At times, attempts to share my faith have not gone so well, while at other moments God has used me to plant seeds of truth in open hearts and even lead people to Christ. Most importantly, I need to obey Jesus' call to go into all the world and preach the gospel (Mark 16:15)—and trust that as I do, He goes before me to prepare hearts and draw men and women to Himself.

If you're not a believer but are sensing a pull in your heart toward trusting in Christ, I encourage you to pray the following prayer. It's not the prayer itself that makes the difference, but rather your complete belief in what you're saying.

> "Lord Jesus ... I want to stop trusting in myself ... and what I can do ... and start trusting in You ... and what You have already done ... when You died for me on the cross. I know that I am a sinner ... and I am sorry for my sins. I ask You to forgive me ... and I invite You to come and live inside of me. I want You to be my Savior ... and my Lord ... which means being #1 in my life. I want to repent and turn away ... from everything You and the Bible call sin ... and I totally commit myself ... to obeying You ... every day, for the rest of my life. Thank You, Jesus."[1]

If you truly believed what you just prayed, then congratulations and welcome into the Family of God! If you have just made a commitment to Christ for the first time, we'd love to hear from you. Please go to my website www.iancbyrd.com, click on the "Contact Ian" button, give us your name and email address, tell us of your decision, and we'll send you some materials to help you in your new walk with Christ.

To grow in your new personal relationship with the Lord, I suggest the following:

1. Spend some time each day praying and thanking God (1 Thessalonians 5:17–18).

2. Daily read the Bible. I suggest beginning with the Gospel of John (1 Peter 2:2).

3. Find a church that teaches the Bible as 100% the Word of God, and encourages a personal relationship with Jesus (Hebrews 10:25).

4. Begin to develop friendships with sincere Christians, and be baptized (1 John 1:7, Romans 6:4).

5. Tell other people about your new relationship with God (Matthew 4:19).[2]

May we always be mindful of our relationship with Christ so that, like my mother, this Scripture will describe our successful life journey:

> *And how blessed all those in whom you live,*
> *whose lives become roads you travel;*
> *They wind through lonesome valleys, come upon brooks,*
> *discover cool springs and pools brimming with rain!*
> *God-traveled, these roads curve up the mountain, and*
> *at the last turn—Zion! God in full view!*
>
> Psalm 84:5–7, MSG

A Final Word

THANK YOU FOR READING *LIFE IS A HIGHWAY*. AFTER HEARing stories from my journey, I hope you realize you're neither alone in your struggles and weaknesses, nor in your moments of restoration and triumph. Life is truly a highway taking us through good times and bad—a road common to us all.

Within these pages, I sought to share principles that have helped me navigate my own journey—a roadmap of sorts to hopefully lead you to the guidance, encouragement, and strength only our loving Heavenly Father can provide. Along with directing the path of your life, the Lord also wants your heart to become a highway, or conduit, for transporting His love and grace to a lost and hurting world. A high calling indeed!

Moving forward, I encourage you to incorporate the principles or truths that particularly stood out in this book. It might be helpful to review specific chapters, and Points to Ponder, where you felt the Lord putting His finger on something in your life, or providing unique encouragement to help you grow in your relationship with Him. Responding to His prompting now will make you a "doer" of the Word, who is blessed in what you do (James 1:23, 25 NKJV).

I also hope you will be inclined to periodically pull this book off the shelf and use it as an encouraging resource when navigating the many twists, turns, valleys, and mountain top experiences marking your life highway in the days and years ahead.

In closing, I want to pray for you one last time before we part company.

"Dear Father, I thank You for the opportunity to share Life is a Highway with this reader—someone so precious and special to You. May he or she truly discover Your strength and embrace the pilgrimage of becoming a road You travel. When his or her life journey descends into a valley of weeping, I ask You to pour out Your grace and comfort so that, in turn, that same comfort can be passed on and invested in others. Thank You that truly "all things work together for good" for those who love You and are called according to Your purpose (Romans 8:28 NKJV). I pray this dear reader would also come to fully know Your unconditional acceptance and loving father's heart—daily sensing Your great pleasure as he or she walks in Your ways and pursues Your purposes. May this child of Yours go "from strength to strength," and ultimately, curve up that heavenly mountain into Your presence, while leaving a tremendous legacy for all those following after. In Jesus' name. Amen."

If this book was a blessing to you,
please consider leaving a review on Amazon
(at *https://amzn.to/2DH00Cc*) and
spreading the word through social media.

Endnotes

CHAPTER 1

1. Baker, Darryl. "Walking by Faith, not by Sight," Weekly Wisdom (blog), March 12, 2012, *http://blogs.christianpost.com/ weekly-wisdom/3-12-12-walking-by-faith-not-by-sight-8681/*

2. Vader Klok, Pastor Duane. Walking by Faith. *http://www.walking byfaith.tv/journal/single-article/128/* (accessed November, 2016).

CHAPTER 2

1. Murray, Andrew. *Wings Like Eagles.* Vereeniging: Christian Art Publishers, 2009.

2. Keathley III, J. Hampton. "Waiting on the Lord." Bible.org. *https://bible.org/article/waiting-lord* (accessed May 11, 2018).

3. Keathley III, J. Hampton. "Waiting on the Lord." Bible.org. *https://bible.org/article/waiting-lord* (accessed May 11, 2018).

4. Keathley III, J. Hampton. "Waiting on the Lord." Bible.org. *https://bible.org/article/waiting-lord* (accessed May 11, 2018).

5. *Dictionary.com*, s.v. "renew," accessed May 11, 2018, *http://www.dictionary.com/browse/renew.*

6. Hampton Keathley III, J. "Waiting on the Lord." Bible.org. *https://bible.org/article/waiting-lord* (accessed May 11, 2018).

7. Morgan, G. Campbell. "Quotable Quotes." Goodreads. *https://www.goodreads.com/quotes/333742-waiting-for-god-is-not -laziness-waiting-for-god-is* (accessed May 15, 2018).

CHAPTER 3

1. Japenqa, Bob. "Introductory Guide to Listening Prayer." Articles, Booklets and Sermons. *https://mtibugs.com/wordpress/articles-booklets -and-sermons* (accessed December 14, 2017).

2. Japenqa, Bob. "Introductory Guide to Listening Prayer." Articles, Booklets and Sermons. *https://mtibugs.com/wordpress/articles-booklets -and-sermons* (accessed December 14, 2017).

3. Japenqa, Bob. "Introductory Guide to Listening Prayer." Articles, Booklets and Sermons. *https://mtibugs.com/wordpress/articles-booklets -and-sermons* (accessed December 14, 2017).

4. Houdman, Michael. "What are the different names of God, and what do they mean?" Got questions. *https://www.gotquestions.org/ names-of-God.html* (accessed December 14, 2017).

CHAPTER 4

1. Webster's 1913, s.v. "set," accessed May 12, 2018, *https://www.websters1913.com/words/Set.*

2. Fine Dictionary, s.v. "resolute," accessed May 12, 2018, *http://www.finedictionary.com/resolute.html.*

CHAPTER 5

1. "Dark Night of the Soul," in *Wikipedia: The Free Encyclopedia*; (Wikimedia Foundation Inc., updated 22 July 2004, 10:55 UTC) [encyclopedia on-line]; available from *https://en.wikipedia.org/wiki/ Dark_Night_of_the_Soul* (assessed May 12, 2018).

2. Thakur, Rajeev. "Promoted to failure? The curious effect of Peter Principle." LinkedIn. *https://www.linkedin.com/pulse/promoted-failure -the-curious-effect-peter-principle-rajeev-thakur* (accessed May 12, 2018).

3. Groth, Aimee. "You're The Average Of The Five People You Spend The Most Time With." Business Insider. *http://www.businessinsider .com/jim-rohn-youre-the-average-of-the-five-people-you-spend-the-most -time-with-2012-7* (Accessed May 12, 2018).

4. Groeschel, Craig. "Creating a Value Driven Culture Pt. 1." *Craig Groeschel Leadership Podcast.* Podcast audio, March 2, 2016. *https://www.life.church/leadershippodcast/creating-a-value-driven -culture-part-1/.*

CHAPTER 6

1. "Somebody's Daughter: A Journey to Freedom from Pornography" documentary. *Christian News Wire. http://www.christiannewswire.com/news/220687783.html* (accessed November 30, 2017).

2. Hosley, Ryan, Steve Watters. "Dangers and Disappointments." Pure Intimacy. *http://www.pureintimacy.org/d/dangers-and-disappointments -of-pornography/* (accessed November 30, 2017).

3. Diamond, Jed. "Your Brain on Pornography." The Good Men Project. *https://goodmenproject.com/featured-content/your-brain-on -pornography-wcz/* (accessed December 7, 2017).

4. Arterburn, Stephen. "10 Steps to Overcoming Pornography Addiction." Growthtrac. *http://www.growthtrac.com/overcoming -pornography-addiction/#.Vb-VdMbF_dl* (accessed November 30, 2017).

5. Rainey, Dennis. "How Do I Escape the Trap of Pornography in My Life?" Family Life. *https://www.familylife.com/articles/topics/life-issues/ challenges/pornography/how-do-i-escape-the-trap-of-pornography-in-my -life* (accessed December 7, 2017).

6. Rainey, Dennis. "How Do I Escape the Trap of Pornography in My Life?" Family Life. *https://www.familylife.com/articles/topics/life-issues/ challenges/pornography/how-do-i-escape-the-trap-of-pornography-in-my -life* (accessed December 7, 2017).

7. Hopler, Whitney. "Break Free of Pornography's Trap." Crosswalk .com. *https://www.crosswalk.com/faith/spiritual-life/break-free-of -pornographys-trap-1210417.html* (accessed December 7, 2017).

8. Enns, Paul. Moody Handbook of Theology (196). As quoted in "Definition of God's Grace." All About. *https://www.allaboutgod.com/ definition-of-gods-grace-faq.htm* (accessed December 7, 2017).

9. Dehass, Ron. *https://www.hedge.org (accessed May 12, 2018).*

10. Fechner, Fritz, Susanna Zdrzalek. "Rewired: How Pornography Affects the Human Brain." Indiegogo. *https://www.indiegogo.com/ projects/rewired-how-pornography-affects-the-human-brain#/* (accessed December 7, 2017).

11. Roberts, Ted. Conquer Series: The Battle Plan for Purity. Dvd Set. *www.conquerorseries.com* (accessed December 7, 2017).

12. Roberts, Ted. *Conquer Series Study Guide*, 80–81. West Palm Beach: Kingdom Works Studios, 2013.

13. Roberts, Ted. "How to Delete Porn from Your Brain." Conquer Series. *https://conquerseries.com/how-to-delete-porn-from-your-brain/* (accessed December 7, 2017).

14. Fox Cabane, Olivia and Judah Pollack. In "How to Delete Porn from Your Brain. Conquer Series. *https://conquerseries.com/how-to-delete -porn-from-your-brain/* (accessed December 7, 2017).

15. Sky Balloon. Rhema. *http://skyballoonstudio.com/rhema/* (accessed May 12, 2018).

16. James, Ken. "How to Deal with your Sexual Addiction." Christian Answers.net. *https://www.christiananswers.net/q-eden/sexaddictiontips .html* (accessed December 7, 2017).

17. Arterburn, Stephen. *Every Man's Battle: Winning the War on Sexual Temptation One Victory at a Time.* New York: The Crown Publishing Group, 2009.

18. Boehi, Dave. "Escaping the Pornography Trap." Growthtrac.com. *https://www.growthtrac.com/escaping-the-pornography-trap/* (accessed May 17, 2018).

19. Arterburn, Stephen. *Every Man's Battle: Winning the War on Sexual Temptation One Victory at a Time.* New York: The Crown Publishing Group, 2009.

CHAPTER 8

1. Maxwell, John C. *Irrefutable Laws of Leadership.* 2nd ed. Nashville. Thomas Nelson. 2007.

2. *Fausset's Bible Dictionary,* s.v. "Baca," accessed May 12, 2018, *https://www.bible-history.com/faussets/B/Baca/.*

CHAPTER 9

1. Kubler-Ross, Elisabeth in Smith, Melinda, Lawrence Robinson, and Jeanne Segal. "Coping with Grief and Loss." Helpguide.org. *https://www.helpguide.org/articles/grief/coping-with-grief-and-loss.htm* (accessed May 12, 2018).

2. Smith, Melinda, Lawrence Robinson, and Jeanne Segal. "Coping with Grief and Loss." Helpguide.org. *https://www.helpguide.org/ articles/grief/coping-with-grief-and-loss.htm* (accessed May 12, 2018).

3. Smith, Melinda, Lawrence Robinson, and Jeanne Segal. "Coping with Grief and Loss." Helpguide.org. *https://www.helpguide.org/ articles/grief/coping-with-grief-and-loss.htm* (accessed May 12, 2018).

4. Smith, Melinda, Lawrence Robinson, and Jeanne Segal. "Coping with Grief and Loss." Helpguide.org. *https://www.helpguide.org/ articles/grief/coping-with-grief-and-loss.htm* (accessed May 12, 2018).

5. Hand, Byron. "Comforting Others with our Comfort Sermon Final." Faithlife Sermons. *https://sermons.logos.com/submissions/44774 -Comforting-others-with-our-comfort-Sermon-Final#content=/ submissions/44774* (accessed May 12, 2018).

6. Cawley, Luke. "Thirty Minutes to a Shareable Testimony." Intervarsity Evangelism. *http://evangelism.intervarsity.org/how/ conversation/30-minutes-shareable-testimony* (accessed May 12, 2018).

7. Reccord, Bob and Randy Singer. *Live Your Passion, Tell Your Story, Change Your World*. Nashville: Thomas Nelson, 2004.

CHAPTER 10

1. Nuyten, John. "Timeline from Abraham to Modern Day Israel." Different Spirit. *http://www.differentspirit.org/resources/timeline.php* (accessed May 12, 2018).

CHAPTER 11

1. Smith, Wendell. *The Roots of Character*. Portland: City Christian Publishing, 1998.

2. Buford, Bob. *Halftime: Moving from Success to Significance*. Grand Rapids: Zondervan, 1997.

CHAPTER 12

1. *The International Standard Bible Encyclopedia*, s.v. "Arabia," as quoted in "Where did Job Live?" Reiterations. *https://reiterations. wordpress.com/2012/07/13/where-did-job-live* (accessed December 15, 2017).

2. Mackay, John. "Job? Who was Job, when did he live, and where did he live?" Ask John Makay. *http://askjohnmackay.com/job-who-was-job -when-did-he-live-and-where-did-he-live* (accessed December 15, 2017).

CHAPTER 13

1. Dawson, John. "The Father Heart of God." Last Days Ministries. *https://www.lastdaysministries.org/Articles/1000008535/Last_Days_ Ministries/LDM/Discipleship_Teachings/John_Dawson/The_Father_Heart .aspx* (accessed December 18, 2017).

2. Dawson, John. "The Father Heart of God." Last Days Ministries. *https://www.lastdaysministries.org/Articles/1000008535/Last_Days_ Ministries/LDM/Discipleship_Teachings/John_Dawson/The_Father_Heart .aspx* (accessed December 18, 2017).

CHAPTER 14

1. Warren, Rick. "Make The Most Of Your Talents." Pastor Rick's Daily Hope. *http://pastorrick.com/devotional/english/make-the-most -of-your-talents* (accessed May 12, 2018).

2. Hailey, Darell. "S.H.A.P.E.: Assessment to Assist in Serving." Timberline Church, Fort Collins, Colorado. *www.iancbyrd.com* (used by permission).

3. Warren, Rick. "Make The Most Of Your Talents." Pastor Rick's Daily Hope. *http://pastorrick.com/devotional/english/make-the-most -of-your-talents* (accessed May 12, 2018).

CHAPTER 15

1. Ngoma, Samuel. *Why is God Silent on Mandela?* Lake Mary: Creation House, 2009, 17.

2. Evans, Marissa K. "Apartheid (1948–1994)." BlackPast.org. *http:// www.blackpast.org/gah/apartheid-1948-1994* (accessed May 12, 2018).

3. A & E Networks. "Nelson Mandela: Champion of Freedom." History. *https://www.history.com/topics/apartheid* (accessed May 18, 2018).

4. "Apartheid," and " Nelson Mandela," in *Wikipedia: The Free Encyclopedia*; (Wikimedia Foundation Inc., updated 22 July 2004, 10:55 UTC) [encyclopedia on-line]; available from *https:// en.wikipedia.org/wiki/Apartheid* and *https://en.wikipedia.org/wiki/Nelson_ Mandela* (accessed Nov 22, 2017).

5. CantyMedia. "South Africa: The New Legal System." *Factba.se. http:// fact.geoba.se/handbookpage.php?id=1405900* (accessed May 12, 2018).

6. Eastwood, C. & Eastwood, C. (2009) *Invictus*. United States:Warner Bros. Pictures.

7. Mandela, Nelson. "Quotable Quotes." Goodreads. *https://www.good reads.com/quotes/278812* (accessed May 12, 2018).

8. Reed, David. "Can Mandela and De Klerk Save South Africa?" in *Reader's Digest*, September, 1990.

9. Mandela, Nelson. "Quotable Quotes." Goodreads. *https://www.good reads.com/quotes/144557* (accessed May 12, 2018).

10. Mandela, Nelson. "Nelson Mandela Quotes." Brainy Quote. *http://www.brainyquote.com/quotes/authors/n/nelson_mandela.html* (accessed May 12, 2018).

11. Seamands, David. *Healing for Damaged Emotions*. Wheaton: Victor Books, 1989, 29-30.

12. ten Boom, Corrie. "Quotes by Corrie ten Boom." Goodreads. *https://www.goodreads.com/quotes/search?utf8=%E2%9C%93&q=Corrie+TenBoom &commit=Search* (accessed May 12, 2018).

13. Fryling, Bob. *Lifeline*. Intervarsity Press, Summer, 1997, as quoted in "What's Good for the Soul." Net Bible. *http://classic.net.bible.org/illustration.php?id=2624* (accessed May 13, 2018).

14. King Jr, Martin Luther. "Martin Luther King Jr Quotes." Goodreads. *https://www.goodreads.com/author/quotes/23924.Martin_Luther_King_Jr_* (accessed May 13, 2018).

CHAPTER 16

1. *Merriam Webster Online Dictionary*, s.v. "accountability," accessed December 18, 2017.

2. Outlaw, Greg. "Christian Accountability." All About God. *https://www.allaboutgod.com/christian-accountability-2.htm* (accessed December 18, 2017).

CHAPTER 17

1. Barnett, Tommy. "Are You Dreaming BIG Enough?" Ministry Today. *http://ministrytodaymag.com/leadership/vision/10649-are-you-dreaming -big-enough* (accessed May 14, 2018).

2. Barnett, Tommy. "Are You Dreaming BIG Enough?" Ministry Today. *http://ministrytodaymag.com/leadership/vision/10649-are-you-dreaming-big-enough* (accessed May 14, 2018).

CHAPTER 18

1. Alcorn, Randy. "Live for the Line, Not the Dot." Eternal Perspectives Ministries. *https://www.epm.org/blog/2014/Dec/17/live-line* (accessed May 14, 2018).

2. Surowiecki, John. "Quotable Quotes." Goodreads. *https://www.goodreads.com/quotes/52041* (accessed May 14, 2018).

CHAPTER 19

1. *Christian Equippers International.* "Are You Going to Heaven? Two Question Test Reveals Answer." South Lake Tahoe, 1981.

2. *Christian Equippers International.* "Are You Going to Heaven? Two Question Test Reveals Answer." South Lake Tahoe, 1981.

About the Author

IAN BYRD IS LEAD PASTOR OF CHURCH OF THE ROCK CALGARY in Alberta, Canada and sits on the Leadership Council of Lifelinks International Fellowship where he provides oversight and input to network churches. Ian has also spoken internationally at ministry training schools and conferences. As a speaker and writer, he has an engaging communication style that helps his audience receive and process challenging truths.

For more information, please visit:

www.iancbyrd.com